LITTLE BOY FOUND

LITTLE BOY FOUND

A LIFE GROWING UP ON THE WEST COAST 1948 ONWARD

PHILIP B PALLETTE

For my Family

INTRODUCTION

My mother was born in Seattle in 1917, but at the time I was born she lived and worked in San Francisco. And she was afraid of a multitude of issues. She was afraid of telling my grandparents she was having an affair, afraid of telling them she was going to have a child. She was terrified of having her lover divorce his barren wife so that he could marry her. Her lover was a prominent and devout Episcopalian. If you know the rules, Episcopal priests could not perform a marriage ceremony involving a divorcee. Here you would have a pair of divorcees, my mother and her lover. Still, my mother had hope.

She knew all about divorce. My mother was a divorcee as of 1944, and she was an alcoholic. She was never a drunk, but she had to have a drink every day. I later learned that I am an adult child of an alcoholic. We now live in a world full of acronyms. An acronym for my condition is ADOC.

Years later, I had to get my birth certificate to get a passport. I received a copy from San Francisco. My birth certificate stated my father was Anthony Pallett, merchant seaman age 34. This was a lie. There was never such a person. My father had falsified my birth certificate.

I am writing this introduction without the aid of an editor. This part of my memoir is thus unedited. It comes straight from my mind and straight from my heart.

CHAPTER 1

SAN FRANCISCO – IN THE BEGINNING

THE HEADLINES **in 1948**

- President Harry Truman ends racial segregation in the U.S. military.
- Margaret Sanger founds the International Planned Parenthood Federation.
- Alfred Kinsey publishes Sexual Behavior in the Human Male.

Okay. In the beginning, I was born. I was told a Sunday morning, after midnight, January 18, 1948. The odd thing was that my own father delivered me. He was not married to my mother. He was an Ob-Gyn and an Endocrinologist. They had had an affair. He was a doctor. She was a lab technician. I have no recollection of this. It went on without my awareness.

. . .

The Headlines in 1950

- Korean War begins when North Korea invaded South Korea in June
- Diner's Club issues the first credit cards.
- Two Long Island commuter trains collide in the Richmond Hills section of Queens killing 79 people
- James Dean gets his break when he appears in a Pepsi Commercial[1]

GEORGIA

I distinctly remember two occurrences. Both were as the result of my walking, hand-in-hand with Georgia, our housemaid in San Francisco at the time. I was later told that Georgia dressed me up in fine clothes. What I do vaguely remember is climbing the steps inside an apartment building with Georgia holding my hand. And I remember walking with Georgia on a sidewalk and looking down at the little square glass vault lights, which are essentially skylights for below-ground illumination. I guess these little glass squares embedded in the sidewalk were allowing sunlight to lighten subterranean spaces.

Anyway, that's what I remember from the year 1950, when I would have been 2 years old. But years later, when I would have been about 15, or so, I accompanied my mother on a visit to the Silverman family living in a suburb home, south of San Francisco. I do not remember much about the visit, except that working in the kitchen was this same woman, Georgia. I went to say hello to her. I recognized her features well. But she was shy and retiring about greeting me. She smiled, and graciously said hello. It turned out that the Silvermans had hired Georgia on a recommendation of my mother some years before.

The Headlines in 1951

- Congress passes 22nd Amendment, limiting a President to two terms.
- Stalin claims the Soviet Union has the atomic bomb.
- Julius and Ethel Rosenberg convicted of passing U.S. nuclear secrets to the Soviet Union; both are sentenced to death.[2]

VASHON ISLAND, WASHINGTON

I remember my grandmother calling it a "peenie." Well, she had raised two boys, and she had had a baby brother, although my grandmother's kid brother had died in 1918 from the famous influenza of that time. She would have been 6 or 7 when he was born, and 10 or so by the time he was a toddler. As for when and how my grandmother picked up the term "peenie," it would be anyone's guess.

Yes, in the summer of 1951, I was transported up to the home of my welcoming grandparents in Vashon Island, Washington. By this time, my grandparents were accustomed to and had accepted the fact of my birth. I think they looked forward to the unique experience that raising a little boy would provide. At this time, I was cute, according to my grandmother.

CHAPTER 2

VASHON ISLAND, WASHINGTON – A LITTLE BOY LOST

THE HEADLINES **in 1952**

- 3300 die of polio in U.S - 57,000 children are paralyzed prior to the widespread use of Polio vaccine
- Thick smog in London on December 4, England causes 4,000 fatalities
- Elizabeth II becomes the Queen of England and the United Kingdom after the death of her father King George VI
- The first Chevrolet Corvette prototype was completed[1]

I LIKED IKE

I was now 4 years old. One thing I remember about 1952—this would have been weeks before the actual election was to take place, is that my sister put a couple of colorized newspaper pictures of the two presidential candidates—side by side and maliciously asked me to pick which one I liked. They were side by side colored renderings of Adlai Stevenson, the Democratic candidate, and Dwight D. Eisenhower, the Republican candidate. Well, our family was a strictly Democrat-voting and supporting family. There was no doubt about whom to support.

I looked at the two pictures, not knowing, being a 4 year-old boy, which was which and which one I should choose. I placed my finger on Eisenhower, and my sister laughed and laughed, again maliciously, saying that I had chosen the wrong person.

Another thing I remember about 1952 was that my grandparents had a special bunk bed constructed for me in the room area adjoining their bedroom. An area set rather far back from their bed location. I remember rather liking the new construction. A special carpenter had come in and built the bunking area for me.

PEEING WITH MY UNCLE BIM

I observed the size of his penis which was considerably larger than my own. My peenie, that is. At the same toilet, on another occasion, I recall defecating into the toilet and my grandfather, who was assisting me at the time, pointed to the fecal matter in the toilet, and said, "Bad!"

HI HO SILVER!

Uncle Bim's house being built down in the bottom of a gulley in Seattle that was difficult to reach by driving, with a gear shift car; a steep hill. I remember there was construction going on, wooden frames and all. I listened to "The Lone Ranger" program on radio and was moved by the music, the Rossini overture to William Tell. I used to run behind the furniture firing my imaginary guns at imaginary bad guys because of what I heard the Lone Ranger doing on radio.

Also, there was "Wild Bill Hickok" starring Guy Madison and Andy Devine. Meanwhile, in the kitchen, my grandmother listened each morning to such shows as "Helen Trent" and "Backstage Wife." Then there was "Queen for a Day" hosted by Jack Bailey.

I think for Christmas, 1952, I received a snow sled. And we had a bit of snow over the winter time on Vashon Island. Around this time I remember my grandparents riding the sled down a slope in our yard and at the bottom of the slope, they kind of rolled off and into the snow. I remember my grandmother laughing and laughing as the ride ended.

CHAPTER 3

VASHON ISLAND – A LITTLE BOY LOVED

———

THE HEADLINES **in 1953**

- Gen. Dwight D. Eisenhower inaugurated President of United States (Jan. 20).
- Julius and Ethel Rosenberg executed in Sing Sing prison (June 19).
- Alleged Communist Charlie Chaplin leaves U.S. for good. Justice Dept. warns him any attempt to reenter the country will be challenged.
- Joseph Stalin dies (March 5).[1]

TCP

On April 24, 1953, my cousin Terry was born. I remember my Uncle Bim, Terry's father, coming to our house in Cove, Washington on Vashon Island, and bringing a tcp sign which he had grabbed from a Shell service station somewhere in Seattle. Tcp was some kind of additive to the gaso-line that the Shell company was promoting. This big colorful tcp sign had a yellow background, and red letters. Of course, tcp stood for Terrance Cumberland Pennell, Terry's actual name.

My best friend in 1953 was Johnny Meyers and he lived next door. His mother, Elsie, was a registered nurse. Johnny had a little brother, Chrissy Meyers, who was about 3 years old at the time. I remember one time when we were out playing in the sunshine. I suddenly felt an extra warmth on my pants leg. I looked down and little Chrissy Meyers was peeing on my pants leg.

WHEN JOHNNY COMES MARCHING HOME AGAIN

We had built what my grandmother called a bulkhead, made of logs and running parallel to the walkway and steps down from the street (actually an unpaved road). One day Johnny Meyers and I were standing up on top of the bulk-head, and Johnny decided to push me off. He did so and I went crashing down landing on my head upon the cement walkway. I suppose I started to cry as I got up, and my grandmother was very concerned. I remember her using the word "concussion" as she sought Elsie Meyers's help. Elsie had me lie down and put an ice compress above my right eye.

During this time we picked blackberries. Blackberries are sweet, almost incomparably sweet in the Pacific northwest. And on Vashon Island in the 1950s, wonderful blackberries grew on vines near our house. These were not what we called wild blackberries, these berries were wild enough. Wild blackberries were smaller. These blackberries were large, plump and sweet. Except for when you got a bad one, somehow infected and foul tasting. But those were rare.

My grandmother used to make wonderful huckleberry jam and for this she had to rely on a woman who lived in the hills of the island and who had access to the bushes of the huckleberries. The woman used to supply my grandmother with the berries, and my grandmother made the jam. Huckleberry jam became a favorite of mine.

When we moved away from Vashon Island, huckleberry jam disappeared forever from my grandmother's repertoire of specialties. Huckleberries are very close cousins to blueberries. And almost as if to compete with the huckleberry jam, my Aunt Irene used to gather raspberries and made wonderful raspberry jelly. Both women made liberal use of paraffin wax to complete their jam or jelly making tasks.

OH SO-SHA

One day, I got acquainted with some children who lived across the street. I knew they had a TV set and I asked them about "Superman" and what it was like. They never asked me up to come and watch, and I doubt my grandmother would have allowed it anyway. There were two children from this family that I remembered. The little boy could not have been more than 3 years old. I remember asking him what his sister's name was. His sister was my age or maybe slightly older. The little boy answered "So-sha." That was her name. "So-sha," he repeated. The little girl looked at me and said, "No, my name is 'Susan.' He just cannot pronounce 'Susan.'"

FIRST GIRL FRIEND

Later that year, as the school year dawned, I entered the Vashon Island Kindergarten. Two things I remember about that. One was a red-haired girl named Virginia, who became my girl friend. I remember being outside and getting on my hands and knees. I said, "I'll be your turtle. Will you be my turtle?" Apparently she thought that was a good idea, because she answered in the affirmative. I also remember the kindergarten play before mothers, and in my case, my grandmother.

ME – THE BIG BAD WOLF

We put on "The Three Little Pigs" and in a way, I was kind of the hit of the show because I played the big, bad wolf. I remember the climactic scene where I had to take out the little pigs. I got down on the floor and rolled like madman across the "stage" and the kids playing the pigs backing hurriedly away in utter terror. The audience, including my grandmother enthusiastically approved of this scenario, and my actions were greeted with much enthusiastic laughter.

BUTCH

The bully of the neighborhood, or should I say, just beyond our neighborhood as the street ended and somewhat further along the way lived Butch and his bad boy brothers and father. One day, my cousins Paul, Lin and Olivia were visiting us. Paul and I ventured out past the end of our street and walked up close to Butch's house. All of a sudden, Butch burst out of the house wielding a knife. Paul and I took off for our place, as fast as we could run. Butch was chasing us. We made it safely to our yard. Butch had red hair and was 8 years-old. I was just 5 and I think Paul was still 7 or 8.

THE NANTHROPS

One night I visited the Nanthrops up the street from our house. Ann Nanthrop and Spike Nanthrop had a nice female Doberman dog named Amber, which was not too friendly with me, as I remember. That was understandable, as I was "an intruder." Spike, a terrific though quiet guy, worked in the city as a riveter or welder for Boeing Aircraft. He lacked personality compared to Ann, who was always vivacious and talking. They say opposites attract.

They had no children, though they desperately wanted them. Ann, as I indicated, was a joyful person with flaming red hair. They really wanted to adopt me, that's the reason I was there, and I believe they tried to enter into negotiations with my mother. Nothing quite came of it, though my grandparents liked the Nanthrops and thought it was a workable solution. The deal breaker for me in this situation was Ann's cooking. She was a terrible cook. The time I went there, they had liver, which I hated. But I politely ate as much as I could, and I never told anyone that Ann was a terrible cook, except maybe my grandmother.

SAMMY, THE ROAD GRATER MAN

For Christmas, 1953, I received a beautiful orange-color toy road grater from Uncle David and Aunt Irene. It was something I had wanted and begged for. That Christmas, I also received a wonderful six shooter cap pistol, with holster and black belt. I was so eager to dress up as a cowboy, I almost wet my pants with excitement. I also got a new Voit softball, though I was yet to really discover baseball. The most memorable gift I got was a little doll whom I named Sam. "Sammy the Road Grater man," I called him. And I put him on top of my new road grater. But, as I remember, my interest in the road grater had peaked, as I could really not put it to practical use.

CHAPTER 4

ST. ANDREWS HOUSE - HOODS CANAL, WASHINGTON

———

THE HEADLINES **in 1954**

- January 14 – Marilyn Monroe marries baseball player Joe DiMaggio at San Francisco City Hall.
- Army v. McCarthy inquiry (Apr. 22–June 17); Senate votes in Dec. to condemn Sen. McCarthy for misconduct.
- In Brown versus Board of Education of Topeka the Supreme Court unanimously bans racial segregation in public schools (May 17).[1]

Although I was still in Kindergarten, I remember one day some of us kindergartners were invited to visit the Vashon Elementary school and sit in on a 1st grade class for an hour or so; perhaps to see how older kids operated. This was interesting for me because in this class was a friend of mine, Brian Crecelius. The Crecelius family lived about a half mile from our house. Grace was the mother, and she was a kind character. She could sing, contralto, at a professional level. Her husband, Chris, was an engineer, and had developed a business, Pacific Industries, which he conducted from a barn next to their house. He made instruments for measuring in the sea, under water.

The Crecelius family had at least 4 children that I can remember. There was Sylvia, who became a close friend of my sister. She must have been 11 or 12 in 1954. Then came Eric, who looked a lot like his father - blonde and sinewy. Then came my buddy, Brian, who I think was about four months older than I was, and resembled his mother in appearance. The day I was invited to the Vashon Elementary School, I remember greeting Brian, and I think he surprised me by being so friendly towards me. And the one activity I remember was when members of his class counted by 2s or 3s or 4s or 5s or 6s up to 100. And I remember Brian participating in this event.

When Uncle David and Aunt Irene brought their kids over, we got together with the Crecelius family. They were wonderful people. One time, we went out on a boat that Mr. Crecelius captained. And then, we camped outside the house in a tent. I remember how I ruined this experience for Eric, as I committed stupidities like dumping food on the grass inside the tent, making co-existence impossible. I think

Eric was not happy with me. I wanted to ruin their perfect little world a bit.

BRIAN AND ERIC

This was too bad because in their workshop, Brian and Eric had made a workable sling shot for me out of wood, nylon tubing and a buckskin pouch in which you could place stones to be fired at birds. I don't remember what happened to this slingshot. Perhaps my grandfather or grandmother took it away from me before I could put somebody's eye out. But before they could take it away from me, I found it worked pretty well.

One day, I don't remember the circumstances, but Brian and I got an axe and in his back yard, we chopped down a small tree. I think I was a little boy who had a tendency to want to destroy. I think I always thought I could put these destroyed items back together. Anyway, Brian's father, Mr. Crecelius soon confronted us and, though he did not punish me directly, he informed my grandfather. And I would not have been surprised if Brian did not receive a whipping from his father.

In January 1954, I had turned six years old. What I remember most about 1954 is that that was the year that we moved from Vashon Island, near Seattle, to Hoods Canal, also near Seattle, but further away. This would have taken place either in the late spring or summer of 1954. My grandfather, being 67, had retired from being the rector at the Vashon Island Episcopal Church.

ST. ANDREWS HOUSE

We moved into St. Andrews House, as part of my grandfather's retirement from the Episcopal priesthood. Bishop Bain maintained a small apartment as part of St. Andrews House, and we had a small apartment there, but the purpose of St. Andrews House was that it served as a seminary retreat for young men about to enter the priesthood. And I remember one period in late 1954 where a flock of these young men came to stay at St. Andrews. We did not stay long in St. Andrews House, an immense, log structure, with rooms on two floors for the young men to sleep in.

Some young men wanted to play with me, but nothing untoward. I went to school there in the Union, Washington Elementary School as a first grader. I made a friend, whose parents ran a sort of resort along the canal. St. Andrews House was across the road from the canal and up a road, a sort of driveway.

There was also a model home right on the canal, not far from where my friend lived. This fancy house made it into Sunset Magazine, and was something to behold at the time to have this modern house right near where we lived.

SEANY DENNY

Yes, the friend I made was named Seany Denny. I do not recall what he looked like, but his mom invited me to come over for lunch one day. I seem to remember the school was next to the little resort that Seany's parents ran. And I remember in school, we made cranberry sauce and I took it home to my grandparents. We also had photographs taken of all the kids in the class, and I took those home, too, but my grandparents did not want to pay for the photos of me. Being a destructive little kid, I stuck a pin through one of the photos at the top edge of the picture so that I could pin it somewhere. This upset my grandmother a great deal because she said now they would have to buy the photographs of me. I still have this photo, though. It sits framed in our living room. My wife liked it and you can still see the little pin hole that I made in 1954 at the top of the photo.

Phil, age 6 - November, 1954 - Hoods Canal
Elementary School photograph.

At St. Andrews House that fall we bought a TV set from Sears Roebuck Company with the brand name of Silver-tone. I remember watching *Life with Elizabeth*, starring Betty White in our living room at St. Andrews House. The announcer, Jack Narr, always asked Betty (Elizabeth) at the end of the show following some mishap, "Elizabeth, aren't you ashamed of yourself?" And Elizabeth would always smile and shake her head, "Uh-uh" she always said. That was young Betty White.

· · ·

Also, on TV that year was the World Series, won in 4 straight games by the New York Giants. Perhaps we bought the TV set after the series was over, as I do not remember watching a single game. I missed Willie Mays's famous catch. Probably I was in school when it happened. I don't remember anything about going to school, except for making the cranberry sauce.

STRIPPING IN THE WOODS

I do remember that near St. Andrews House there lived some people, in particular, an older kid and this young 5 year-old girl. The three of us were in the woods not far from St. Andrews House, and the older kid asked me to take off my pants and expose myself. He also asked the little girl to lower her panties and show herself, we both exposed our genitalia and I remember looking at hers and nothing registering to me. I do not remember the older boy's name nor the girl's name.

We have a commemorative photo which is also in my living room today. That summer at St. Andrews House. It shows us, my grandparents, my sister and I, my mother, my Aunt Gladys (my grandmother's sister), and 19 year-old Bob Habeeb. Taking the picture, I am sure, was Martin Allison (known then as "Marty"), who had been my mother's San Francisco roommate, and an enthusiastic amateur photographer. I think she still was my mother's roommate at the time of this photo.

A Family gathering of sorts. Bob Habeeb is leaning into the camera. My mother is second from the right, my grandmother extreme left.

My mother, Marty and Bob were all up from San Francisco on vacation. Bob came along because my mother was sort of mentoring him. As for Aunt Gladys's husband, Uncle Ernst, who was a professional photographer, I do not know why he was not in the picture. Knowing him, he was probably off exploring the woods or the house, or possibly even the canal itself. In the picture, my mother, my Aunt Gladys and my grandmother are all smoking. That is what they did in those days.

OLD GOLD AND OTHER BRANDS

My grandmother's brand was strictly Pall Mall, which she called Pell Mell. And to this day, I am not entirely sure that that is not the correct pronunciation of Pall Mall. My mother always smoked Philip Morris. I don't remember what Aunt Gladys smoked but her older sister Winnifred always smoked Old Gold. People in those days seemed to swear by the brand they chose. My Aunt Eleanor, Terry's mom, smoked dual filter Tarryton and her husband, my Uncle Bim smoked Camels. My Uncle David smoked Chesterfields. Grandpa did not smoke. Nobody I knew smoked Lucky Strike, but I am certain millions of people did.

I also vaguely remember that my grandfather and my Uncle Edgar, who had been born and raised in Liverpool, England, went down to swim in the canal and they picked up some oysters. They ate the oysters and got sick as dogs. Yeah, they threw up.

PRETENDING TO BE NICE IN SHELTON, WASHINGTON

Also, one day, I went in the car with this reputedly rich lady to the nearest large city: Shelton, Washington. This lady did not have children of her own, and I think I remember my grandmother telling me to behave myself and be kind to this well-dressed, wealthy woman. She was, as I vaguely remember, wearing a hat. Ladies did wear hats in those days, if they emanated from the fashion-conscious days of the 1940s. This woman drove me to Shelton and bought me an ice cream soda or something. I did not like malted milk, so we avoided malted milk. I do not think I made the lady happy, but she drove me home and that was that.

Here in the St. Andrews House woods, I seem
to be saying to the photographer "How do you
want me now, Marty?" 1954

I do remember my grandmother catching me drinking water out of the faucet in the bathroom, because the water was cold and good. But I suffered from bed-wetting at the time, and my grandmother was trying to prevent me from loading up with "the cold stuff" as she called it. I think she got sick and tired of having to wash my pee-soaked sheets every day. My grandmother was to turn 61 that September 5, 1954.

CHAPTER 5

EDMONDS, WASHINGTON – SARGE THE DOG

THE HEADLINES **in 1955**

- Jonas Salk's polio vaccine is declared safe and effective
- "The Mickey Mouse Club" debuts on ABC.
- The Soviet Union and its Eastern Bloc allies sign the Warsaw Pact
- Rosa Parks, an African-American bus passenger, is arrested after refusing to give up her bus seat to a white passenger
- "The $64,000 Question" the popular US television game show starts.[1]

POLIO SHOTS

By 1955 we still lived in Hoods Canal. Somewhere along the line, I received the Jonas Salk vaccine against polio. I was in a classroom, and a doctor wearing a white lab coat administered the shots. I think I had three shots on three occasions. The shots did not hurt because I consciously let my arm go as limp as possible.

After the school year that summer, we moved to Edmonds, Washington. We still had the 1954 green Chevy sedan that my grandfather had bought while we lived on Vashon Island. A manual shift car, a model 2-10. I think we moved to Edmonds because my Aunt Winnifred and Uncle Edgar lived there, right in the town itself. Our house, was up a side street off of the Edmonds Road, which led to the four-lane Aurora highway, which was the highway you took to get to Seattle itself.

A MEMORABLE TRIP

In the summer of 1955 my mother flew up from San Francisco to visit us, and we took an automobile trip to Eastern Washington. We had received a 1955 Chevrolet on loan from the local dealer. Wow, what a car. Practically brand-new. In Eastern Washington we visited the Grand Coulee Dam. My grandmother, stayed home and did not make the trip with us.

We visited the Yoshino family. The older Yoshinos had emigrated from Japan in the late 1920s or 1930s and became sugar beet farmers. I am not sure when, but they joined the Episcopal church, and my grandfather was the Episcopal priest who welcomed them. My grandmother at one point saved the life of one of the Yoshino children, who was about to drown in some pool or lake. I know that Mr.

and Mrs. Yoshino never forgot what my grandmother had done, and the welcoming kindness of my grandfather. I think the boy's name was Elmer. They had a daughter named Louise. I remember her being beautiful with long black hair and golden skin, and having a young family of her own which I visited.

The Yoshinos were kind to me. I still wet their bed. I remember Mrs. Yoshino dressed in a Japanese robe-like kimono garment, and kneeling down to play an ancient Japanese guitar-like instrument. I believe that was the night I wet their bed.

I had turned 7 years old by this time. Edmonds itself was a ferry boat town, like Vashon Island had been, so whenever we went to visit Aunt Winnifred and Uncle Edgar, I could walk down to the ferry dock and see the Nisqually, which was one of the sister ships originally built in the San Francisco Bay area around 1927.

I WAS REALLY INTERESTED IN FERRIES

There were six sister ships: the Nisqually, the Quinalt, the Illahee, the Klikitat, and I cannot recall the two others. But these were wonderful boats, the super ferries of their time; steel hulled, fast and powerful. They held 80 cars each on a single deck. When the San Francisco authorities built their two bridges, the Oakland Bay Bridge and the Golden Gate Bridge in 1936-37, Washington State bought many of the San Francisco ferry boats, which, due to the new bridges, had become obsolete on San Francisco Bay. The state of

Washington renamed nearly all these boats, repainted them white with green trim, and took out the square windows, replacing them with portholes.

They had wooden-hulled boats, too, slower and some still with their square windows; the Klahanee, the Chetzamoka, the Keloken. Then the steel hulled steam driven ferries built in the same San Francisco Bay yard as the Illahee. These boats were smaller and built in 1922; the Shasta and the San Mateo. For some reason, Washington State did not rename these two steam-powered boats, with their enormous smokestacks.

AND BASEBALL

About this time, I had become interested in baseball. My grandfather had played it and my grandmother was a big fan. That fall, I do remember watching the World Series. My grandmother loved the Dodgers, because the Dodgers had given black players a chance to play. Following her, I learned to love the Dodgers and hate the Yankees. My sister, Phoebe, for some reason, loved the Yankees.

In 1955, the Dodgers won the World Series, and I was so happy. My favorite player was Duke Snider. I will never forget him as long as I live. When Duke hit the second of his two home runs in one of those week-end games, I was so thrilled. My sister, Phoebe, was so pissed, she referred to Duke Snider as "Spook Spider." I will never forget that, either.

· · · ·

About this time that I picked up a bat and began slamming the softball that I received from Aunt Gladys and Uncle Ernst back when I was 5 years old, during the Christmas of 1953. I would slam the ball from our driveway up across the little road by our house and into the bank across the street. Then I would walk up the driveway, across the little street, retrieve the ball, walk back and slam the ball up the same direction again.

I did this continuously for hours and I never got tired of it. The ball was a Voit softball given me by Aunt Gladys and Uncle Ernst back when I was 5 years old, during the Christmas of 1953. I would slam the ball from our driveway up across the little road by our house and into the bank across the street. Then I would walk up the driveway, across the little street, retrieve the ball, walk back and slam the ball up the same direction again. I did this continuously for hours and I never got tired of it.

SARGE

My best friend in this neighborhood was Johnny Clifton, an American Indian boy my age, whose tribe I never learned. And a neighbor's dog, named Sarge. Sarge and I roamed the woods together behind our house. I think part of the bargain of Sarge being such a friend to me was that my grandmother was not opposed to feeding Sarge whatever table scraps were available at the time.

But Sarge and I, my goodness, he was such a wonderful dog and companion. He was nearly a full sized German Shepherd mix. And he spent more time with me than he did with his owners, whom I never met. These neighbors also had another dog, a little white dog named Major. But I never had anything to do with Major. Years later, I came to the realization that the owners must have been an Army family, with the male head of the household having been supposedly a Sergeant Major. That is how the dogs came to be named, although this is an unverified supposition on my part.

One time I tried to use some judo moves I had seen on TV. My partner was Johnny Clifton. I tried throwing him by pulling on his arm. This resulted in a yowl of great pain on the part of Johnny Clifton, and I never tried that again. I did not want to hurt my friend.

THE FAIRY WAS NOT A FERRY

I began to go to school. I was now in the 2nd grade and for some reason, during recess, the kids all looked up to me as their leader. I was at this public school, which, by the way, was brand-new that year. We also had a young school teacher, a nice young lady. Apart from remembering how new the desks were in the new classrooms, I remember an exercise conducted by this teacher. She put her hands together and told everyone that a little fairy, like Tinker Bell, was in her hands.

And then she went to each person in the class and, upon opening her hands a bit so each child could peek inside, asked each person "Do you see the fairy?" I remember the little girls in the class said that, "Yes'," they saw the fairy. When the teacher came to me and opened her hands, I did not see anything, but I said, "Yes, I see it." There were members of the class who said they did not see the fairy. I do not remember who they were, but I reported the whole incident to my grandmother.

My grandmother, who was piloting my education, wanted me to skip a grade and move up to the third grade. Apparently the local school system rejected that idea. And it so happened that Rich Whitman School, a private school run by a man named Rich Whitman, was not far from where we lived. My grandmother took steps to transfer me there, and there I could skip a grade and be placed in the third grade. This she had done with her oldest son, David, back in 1922 in Ellensburg, Washington.

HIT BY A CAR

But before that happened, once incident sticks out in my mind from the fall of 1955. I remember how we rode what I thought was a fancy new and powerful school bus back then. I remember the driver was an older guy with glasses, and I was impressed with how he steered the vehicle. The engine was in the back, unlike the older school buses.

One day the bus stopped at our stop, right in front of Rudy's Market, which was at the foot of the road/street on which I lived. This kid, whose name I cannot recall, got off the bus and ran in front of the stopped bus, but got hit by a car which had been behind the bus. The car had pulled out and was attempting to speed past the stopped bus. This is illegal now, but back then, it probably wasn't. I remember the kid was wearing a buckskin jacket with tassels across the front. This was a time of the Davy Crockett craze, because Walt Disney had produced a TV series on Davy Crockett that everybody watched. Every kid wanted a Davy Crockett raccoon hat, or a buckskin suit of some kind.

This kid had his buckskin jacket, he was wearing black loafer shoes and glasses. And when I got off the bus, I saw this kid sprawled on his back on the highway — a two lane highway back then — and the bus driver and the driver of the car bending over him to see how hurt he was. It turned out, the kid was not hurt at all, and got up and continued home, wherever that was. Apparently the driver had slammed on his brakes, honking his horn, well in time so that the kid was knocked over, but not hurt.

MUMBO JUMBO TIMBUKTU

Anyway, I was soon ensconced in Rich Whitman school. I think my grandfather drove me there, as he knew Rich Whitman from somewhere way back in the past. It turned out that Rich Whitman had written a children's song which won a contest in 1923 in Chicago, as the best children's song of the year 1923. I can still remember part of this song.

CHARLIE BROWN

The Brown family lived across the street from our Edmonds house. The Brown's had a fancy driveway, and they had a kid older than I was named Charles. Charles also attended Rich Whitman School, and his mother learned that my grandmother was a pretty good tutor of English. Mrs. Brown engaged my grandmother to tutor Charles. Mrs. Brown also provided my grandmother with books.

My grandmother determined that I was much smarter than Charles, who was a taciturn boy, a boy whom I never saw smile. My grandmother had me read from the books Mrs. Brown had provided. One of the stories in one of the books was about Sacajawea, the Indian guide for Lewis and Clark. In the Rich Whitman classroom, I spoke up about my having this book about Lewis and Clark and Sacajawea. Charles Brown looked at me with pure hatred. Not long after this incident, my grandmother's tutoring days came to an abrupt conclusion.

BARBARA

I remember about my time at Rich Whitman. This was the first time I had a teacher whose name I recall. Her name was Mrs. Franklin, and her main ability was in handwriting, or penmanship. As it turned out, I am a born sloppy writer. My penmanship was horrible. But I learned all the little exercises that Mrs. Franklin taught us, and did my best writing ovals.

Here I was, now a third-grader, younger than all my fellow third-graders. I seemed to excel in Geography, as I remember. And with that, I fell in love with another third-grader named Barbara. I think I worshiped her, and she became my pillow at night, with whom I had whispered conversations. My grandfather, who shared my sleeping quarters, would whisper at me to "Lie still!" or some such command. And 'Barbara' and I would have to quiet down.

I cannot leave 1955 without relating the TV shows that began to dominate my time. In the past, back to 1952 and 1953, I had listened to radio shows that I liked, such as "The Shadow" or "Mr. Chameleon." These were admittedly scary shows, and on Saturday mornings, I would listen to "Big John and Sparky" which came from Cincinnati, Ohio.

But in 1955, I watched Stan Borensen playing his accordion and singing on channel 5, KING TV, Seattle. I can remember him singing the KING's TV clubhouse with Stan song. My grandmother forbade me to watch anything past 9 PM. I do remember watching Davy Crockett each week, as well as Mary Martin as Peter Pan in a major television presentation. There were so many shows to watch, like "Panic" which terrified me.

THE WONDER DOG

One final memory that sticks out. We had a Christmas play at Rich Whitman. I seem to remember that I was dressed in a crape paper costume resembling Robin Hood. The Robin Hood TV series starring Richard Greene, was prominent in our minds at the time, so I was delighted to wear the costume. I was still 7 years old. My grandparents and my sister all came to the show, and I was proud of that. I don't remember a single detail of the show, but what I distinctly remember was our drive home; in the '54 Chevy and snowing heavily. Snowing so much that we could not drive up the road to our house, but had to park in Rudy's supermarket parking lot, which was practically a stone's throw away from our house.

But the way to our house was uphill, and so we got to the foot of the hill and started to trudge up through the snow. Out of the darkness up ahead we heard a sound, then the pounding of foot beats, and then seemingly from nowhere, here was Sarge greeting us. My grandmother was happy, probably my grandfather and sister were begrudgingly happy. I was delirious with joy that Sarge would sense our being there from a great distance away and that he would come running down to greet us. This became one of the most unforgettable moments of my lifetime.

CHAPTER 6

CALIFORNIA, HERE I COME –
LOOKING FOR A HOME

———

THE HEADLINES **in 1956**

- Nikita Khrushchev, First Secretary of USSR Communist Party, denounces Stalin's excesses (Feb. 24).
- Morocco gains independence from France (March 1) and Spain (April 7).
- Workers' uprising against Communist rule in Poland is crushed (June 28-30).
- Egypt takes control of Suez Canal (July 26). Israel launches attack on Egypt's Sinai peninsula and drives toward Suez Canal (Oct. 29). British and French invade Egypt at Port Said (Nov. 5). Cease-fire forced by US pressure stops British, French, and Israeli advance (Nov. 6).
- Soviet troops and tanks crush anti-Communist uprisings in Hungary (November).[1]

The year 1956 came and saw me still at Rich Whitman School. I was still in the third grade, and much in love with Barbara. The worst thing that happened to me was in the swimming class at Rich Whitman. They had a licensed Red Cross swimming teacher, a kind woman in her thirties with short hair named Terri, and all us kids were asked to get into the pool for a swimming lesson. Well, I don't remember what happened, but apparently Terri asked me to put my head in the water and float or swim from point A to point B. And I got terrified to the point where I had hysterics. I remember the word because that was what they said I had. I was shaking and sitting in the dressing room and excused from all future swimming lessons.

That year, roller skating became a bit of a craze at the school and soon, I became the dominating roller skater in the school. The school was a single building surrounded by a cement walkway, ideal for skating. I had the best roller skates available at the time.

In those days, we would fasten them to our shoes with a key to tighten the metal grips. I could beat everyone with a speed race, and one day I remember I fell and scraped my arm. A little girl watched this happen and responded to her friend, "God, he's brave." I never thought of myself as brave. I liked the speed of the skating.

. . .

One spring weekend, Uncle David and Aunt Irene arrived with their kids at our home in Edmonds, and they brought Paul's bicycle, Lin's bicycle and even Olivia's tricycle. They must have owned a VW bus at that point to be able to fit all those vehicles. Anyway, soon we were riding the bikes on the extensive driveway, over which I had become accustomed to slamming my softball.

INJURY TIMEOUT

We continued to ride, including my sister, Phoebe, on her girls bike, which was green and had the center bar lower down so that girls could sit and access the pedals more than on a "boys" bike. I had this bike given me by my grandfather whereby I could not reach the pedals, since the center was bar higher up, so that even if I didn't sit on the seat, but stood up, I could not pedal the bicycle. I rode Paul's smaller red bike, the pedals of which I could reach. Paul, being older, could reach the pedals, and he rode my bicycle so that all were riding around the driveway.

Everything was going great, and I was having so much fun when I caused a great ruckus, bringing the otherwise happy event to a close. Riding freely on Paul's bike, I crossed in front of my sister, who, to avoid hitting me, put on the brakes so hard that she fell into the space of the lower bar on her green girls bike.

The handle bar swung around and struck her hard in the throat, causing her to break into tears, sounding the alarm. She was apparently injured. No, as it turned out, she was able to breathe. The fear was that the handlebar had damaged her windpipe. But the result was that the biking fun on the driveway ended with this calamity.

Also, on another visit from Uncle David's family, Paul and I were out back on the edge of the woods, throwing rocks. I found this one rather flat, sharp-edged rock that I was going to throw sidearm. I reached back and in my throwing motion, the rock, still in my hand, struck Paul in the back of his head. This caused a little bleeding and Paul ran bawling into the house. Paul was older than I. It shocked me to hear him cry for the first time, the one time in my memory.

I followed Paul into the house, and I was so afraid that Uncle David would beat me, that I also began to cry. The words I remember speaking to this day. "The rock never left my hand. The rock never left my hand." Out of fear, I began having hysterics so that, my grandmother poured out a cup of port wine for me to drink. I vaguely remember drinking it, and it seemed to stop my hysterics. Paul had also stopped crying.

THE OLD PRO, ELWOOD AND FALSTAFF BEER

One thing about 1956 would be the baseball broadcasts on Saturdays, The Game of the Week. This was always featuring Dizzy Dean and Buddy Blattner at the microphone. I can specifically remember one game where ol' Diz was broadcasting and Al Kaline of the Detroit Tigers went back and either caught or retrieved a ball in right field.

· · ·

He then went to throw the ball back into the infield and as he drew his arm back to throw, his wrist bumped into the outfield railing, and knocked the ball loose. He had to pick it up again and throw it. I remember Dizzy Dean saying something like, "Fans, you saw there on your screen how the right fielder Kaline drew back to throw and lost the ball." I am thinking now that CBS broadcast this game from either New York or Boston, the fields of which would have had such a railing out in right field.

Another game I remember my hero, Duke Snider, running in to make a shoestring catch, missing it, and the ball going underneath his glove back towards the outfield wall. The games from the East Coast all seemed to come to our West Coast location at 10 AM or 11 AM. That was because of the difference in time zones.

UNEXPECTED VISTORS

One day I came home from school and learned there had been a great fire at my Uncle David's house in Seattle. Everyone survived. But I remember visiting the house on 19th Avenue northeast, a house that I was familiar with because I often visited there. And the garage had burned down, the kitchen was damaged. I can still remember seeing the orange deep fryer they had, melted. And the smell of burnt wood. I can still smell it to this day. Something I will never forget.

The upshot was, my grandparents offered to put up Uncle David, his wife and three children in our Edmonds house.

Not a horrible commute for Uncle David, though I don't know how he got to work in Seattle. With an MA in English from the University of Oregon, he worked primarily as a writer / editor for the City Light publication, Argus.

But this is a digression from my topic. To return to my memories of 1956, one thing I recall is that before the house fire in Seattle, my grandmother was unwell for a period, about two weeks. And during this time, I got to live with Uncle David, Aunt Irene and the three kids, Paul, Lin and Olivia. I was happy with this situation. The bonus was that the girl I was crazy about, Barbara, lived in Seattle. And my Aunt and Uncle's house was on the same mini-bus route that took Barbara to her house.

HEAVEN

Also, I sat next to Barbara in the front seat, and the driver, who by that time was used to Barbara, asked her if I, meaning me, was bothering her. If so, said the driver, I would have to move to another seat. "No", said Barbara. "He's nice to talk to." So the driver was satisfied, and attended to his driving from Rich Whitman to Seattle. And I was thrilled. Barbara actually liked me!

I think that summer, Rich Whitman offered a summer school. My grandfather was offered a position as a teacher. I remember Mrs. Franklin was teaching that summer, as well. She asked me, "Do you want to be in my class, or do you want to be with your grandfather?" I replied after a bit of thinking, "I think I would rather be with my grandfather." I sensed that Mrs. Franklin was somewhat disappointed in this answer, because my grandfather was a lousy teacher.

My grandfather started teaching us French. I remember he was using the method taught him when in 1917 the YMCA sent him for three months of French language training to Princeton University. I remember his teaching us to say, "No" in French. He pronounced it "Naw" and indicated we should say it through our nose.

Another day, my grandfather was teaching us baseball. He was pitching. In those days, my grandmother referred to my grandfather as being "lame". That is, he had a bad hip, and this required a hip replacement. But back then, he merely limped a bit. He was 69 years old that summer, and at 16 years of age, back in 1903, he was signed to a professional baseball contract. He might have made a career out of it except he was 90% blind in one eye.

Anyway, I remember stepping up to the plate and my grandfather was pitching. This was softball, not baseball. And my grandfather who had organized softball games for years, pitched me one right over the plate. I swung and hit the ball squarely, a line drive headed right past his left side. My grandfather reached a bare hand up and grabbed the line drive like nothing, and I was out. I will never forget that big paw reaching up and grabbing what would have been a sure hit.

· · ·

In the fall of 1956 I experienced another lasting memory. Rich Whitman himself had a large TV set on a rolling table/cart so that he could watch a game of the 1956 World Series. I remember this was in the same room where my grandfather had tried to teach us French. Sort of cafeteria room, I think. Anyway, the picture on the TV, black and white of course, was clear, and they had a close up of the Dodgers playing in Ebbets Field in Brooklyn, New York, and the pitcher Clem Labine coming in to relieve whomever the starter had been. This is all I remember from this moment, but I do remember Rich Whitman and some boys gathered around the TV set to watch.

As for my grandparents and me, we moved into the garage, which my grandparents had converted into living space. They also bought lots of new clothes for the kids, because their clothes were pretty much smoke drenched. I remember living in the garage, where I slept, etc. I do remember we had a small pool table, where I sort of learned how to shoot pool. All this seemed to prompt our move down to the San Francisco area, a suburb of San Francisco called Mill Valley, in Marin County. When you go across the famous Golden Gate Bridge, you are in Marin County.

CALIFORNIA HERE I COME

I vaguely remember being on the train from Seattle to Oakland California with my grandmother. I remember eating a cheese sandwich on board the train. And I remember we got on a ferry boat in Oakland and took the trip across San Francisco Bay to San Francisco itself. Let's see, I was 8 years old at the time.

.   .   .

My grandmother always disliked California. Her birth occurred in Fergus Falls, Minnesota, and she had lived in the Seattle area for 60 years or so, I think moving to Seattle from Minnesota in 1897 or so as a 3 or 4 year-old child. She became pro Washington State, pro Washington Huskies football, and loved the fact the University of Washington football team welcomed black players like George Fleming and Ray Jackson.

She loved the Brooklyn Dodgers baseball team and players like Roy Campanella and Jackie Robinson. My grandmother liked to watch boxing matches and always rooted for the black boxer to knock the white guy on his behind. And my Grandmother, Isabel, was a character. Hard, hard physical labor, drinking booze, and smoking would end up killing her prematurely in November 1960. To me, she was more of a mother to me than my actual mother. She was Grandma.

Also, and this lingers back to 1954 and earlier, I had become close to my cousin Paul. Actually, all three of my cousins, David and Irene's children, I was pretty close to them. Paul was about 2 1/2 years older than I was. Then came Lin, who was about 6 months younger than I. came Olivia, the baby of the family, who was about 2 1/2 years younger than I was. My other cousins were Jay and Terry. I was not as close to them because my grandparents did not like their mother, Eleanor, who had married their youngest son, Bimbo. Well, Aunt Eleanor called him John, or Johnny, as John was his proper name. "Bim" was his nickname that my grandparents always used. Short for "Bimbo," which was sort of short for the Italian "bambino." My grandmother loved the name, and my Uncle "Bim" disliked the name.

PINELLA TO PENNELL

I looked up all these records from 1917 through the 1920s and my grandfather was still legally John Pinella, as he was from Philadelphia of Naples immigrant parents. John Pinella legally changed his name to John Pennell around 1927, when he belatedly, at the age of 40, entered the Episcopal priesthood.

But interesting to note is that my mother, born in 1917, was baptized as Mary Elizabeth Pinella. The kids in 1927 were all changed to last name Pennell. But my Uncle Bim, somewhat coincidently, was actually born in Trento, Italy in 1921, as John Pinella. And my grandmother had traveled from Seattle in late 1919 to join my grandfather, first in southern France, and then in northern Italy. My grandmother was excited to be traveling to Europe, and she never forgot the experience.

It should be noted that the original birth records for Bim were supposedly burned in a fire, and so Bim remained an Italian citizen until sometime in the mid 1930s. And with the anti-fascist movement in the United States at that time, Uncle Bim had some miserable experiences at school.

Back during this time, my grandmother often told the story of when Bim was a child. One day he came up to my grandmother, his mother that is, and said to her, "Some human beans are at the door." So my grandmother went to see who was visiting her, opened the front door and saw no one. But on the welcome mat in front of the door were dried white beans. My grandmother often told me this story, and thought the whole thing hilarious.

MILL VALLEY RESIDENTS

By the end of 1956, we were living in this beautiful new house in California, fancy, my mother, my grandparents and Marty (Allison Martin) all living together and pitching in with the mortgage payments. The memories I have of living there in Mill Valley, California. Well, first of all there was Elvis Presley, whom I did not care for, singing "Don't be Cruel" and "Hound Dog". My favorite song of the time was "Singin' the Blues" by Guy Mitchell. Another favorite of mine was "Walkin' in the Rain" by Johnny Ray.

The house we lived in was modern and was situated at the base of Mount Tamalpais. It had a push button talk system so anyone coming to the house would have to talk electronically with a person inside the house. To get to the Mill Valley School, which I now attended, I had to leave this house, walk a short distance through a forest of giant redwoods and there was the school across the street.

One night at this fancy new house, Marty's nephew Paul came to dinner. He had a blonde beautiful girl with him as a date. I remember Paul as a partially balding dark-haired young guy who was a junior executive for some hotel. And I remember Paul out in the kitchen afterwards necking with this beautiful blonde girl, who had her shoes off and was in nylons. She and Paul were doing the dishes, as I would find out that the house was not modern enough to have a dish washing machine at that time.

I had started the 4ᵗʰ grade at Rich Whitman School, still in Edmonds in 1956, and I remember the teacher's name was Miss Prince. And one of the girls in the class asked her "Can we call you Princess?" I don't remember the teacher's response, but in that classroom, for the first time I got to use a ballpoint pen. This was something entirely new for me, and I scribbled away.

Later, having transferred down to the Mill Valley School, continuing with the 4ᵗʰ grade, my teacher's name was Mrs. Hildebrandt. She was a kind spinster-like woman. I would never want to say something that would hurt her. I greatly liked and respected her. I remember once at a softball game, I spit off to the side of the plate, and Mrs. Hildebrandt chided me for spitting. "We don't spit here." Or some words to that effect.

A NEW BARBARA

In that school, I took a liking to a well-built girl, well-proportioned I'd like to say, who also happened to be named Barbara. Then there was this kid named Hank, whom I sat behind. I remember for some reason I snuck behind Hank and sniffed his pants. Sorry admission, but it did happen. Much more in my memory was a fat kid who was certainly a bully of the class, and his name was Dicky DeBeaubien. His father was well-known at that time in Mill Valley as the owner of the DeBeaubien car dealership. And, there was Bruce. I came to realize that Bruce and Barbara were sort of an item. And that Dicky DeBeaubien was sweet on Barbara himself and strove to make Barbara his girl friend.

In that elementary school, the most important game we played was fashioned after baseball, but called kickball. The way they played the game, and in none of the other schools I attended was this done, there was a pitcher and the pitcher rolled a rubberized soccer ball to home plate. And the batter, or I should say, the kicker, would run up and kick the ball. In our class, Dickie DeBeaubien was among the best kickers. Perhaps slightly better, was Bruce. They would both kick the ball far out into the outfield area.

The game was always played before school and anyone could play. If some guy caught a kicked ball on the fly, that guy would be the next kicker up. One day, I was out in the field and a fly ball came out near me. I could have caught and become the next kicker, but I let the ball fall to the ground and whoever, rounded the bases. The kicker of a successful kick like that ran the risk of somebody throwing the ball at him. And if someone hit him with the ball and his foot was not on one of the bases, the guy was retired.

CHARLIE'S IN THE ALLEY!

There was this one kid named Charlie. He was smaller than most, but he could kick like a monster. In those days, the boys seemed unaware of what their European and South American brethren well knew, that if you kicked the ball with the side of your foot, you could meet greater distance. Nobody did this, as these American boys all used the example of the top football field goal kickers, such as Gordy Soltau, or Lou Groza, or Sam Baker who all kicked straight on with their toes to the ball.

In that schoolyard, directly away from home plate, in what might be called the center field area, there arose a cement bulkhead, which supported another yard above the main schoolyard. This small schoolyard apparently contained swings, slides, and merry-go-rounds; something for the little kids to enjoy. And then running parallel to the distant cement wall heading away from home plate was the wall of the school itself. There was a sort of alley way between this cement wall and the school.

I remember it well that one day, some big guy came up to kick and some outfielders started shouting, "Charlie's in the alley! Charlie's in the alley!" As if to inform the kicker that if he kicked a long one which made it out to the alley, Charlie was there to catch it and if Charlie caught it, the kicker was out.

Charlie somehow managed to "steal" my baseball glove. And Hank, whom I told about this, caught up with Charlie in some store around the school. He had my glove, and Hank made him give it back to me. I think I had written something on the strap of the glove which served as an identifying mark. Charlie raised no fuss, but handed the glove back to me.

CHIEF PHOTOGRAPHER

In San Francisco that autumn, I attended with my mother a christening of baby Jamie Mitchell. This took place in an Episcopal church, probably All Saints Episcopal church. I knew the Mitchell family. They were friends of the Hensleys from church. Anyway, there I was, an 8-year-old boy with my primitive Brownie camera, sitting in the back seat of somebody's car, and through the glass window of the car, I saw Kennth Mitchell amongst a crowd of people, holding baby Jamie and peering out towards us. I snapped a picture, not knowing what else to do.

Years later, that picture of Ken holding baby Jamie appeared in a blown up version on the living room wall of the Mitchell's San Francisco home. Ken maintained that this was the one picture taken of the event that he had. I was somewhat amazed that a picture taken by an 8 year-old kid through a car window on a cheap Brownie camera would have amounted to that much importance.

NIGHT LIGHTS

During that brief time in that beautiful house in Mill Valley, I slept in a large closet. I did not mind sleeping in there. With all the residents, bedrooms were scarce. For the first time, I had the room, the large closet that is, to myself. I also had this small brown Bakelite radio to which I always listened. I had it tuned to KSFO, and the music I remember is that of Sammy Davis Jr. singing "Some People Gamble with Matchsticks, Others Gamble with Gold" and Nat King Cole singing "Night Lights".

But the house arrangement was not working. I mean the house with all those folks contributing to the mortgage on the house. First of all, my grandmother was unhappy. Winter and there was no garden for her. She took after her great old cousin, Luther Burbank, the famous botanist of the nineteenth century, and after whom I attained my middle name of "Burbank." My grandmother loved to garden. She loved flower gardens, vegetable gardens. She had always had at least one or the other. In Mill Valley, she had nothing. I remember her being cranky one day, and I yelled that I hated her. I remember being on the polished new wooden steps, and she I think had a vacuum cleaner in her hands.

CHAPTER 7

MILL VALLEY, CALIFORNIA – THAT'S MY HOME?

———

THE HEADLINES **in 1957**

- USSR launches Sputnik 1 on inaugurating the Space Age and the Space Race
- The final new episode of the classic television comedy "I Love Lucy" aired on CBS
- The popular Philadelphia television show "American Bandstand" makes its national television debut
- Movies included "Twelve Angry Men" and "The Bridge Over the River Kwai", and TV showed "Perry Mason" and "Maverick" for the first time.[1]

On January 19 of 1957, I remember telling Mrs. Hildebrandt in the Mill Valley School that yesterday had been my birthday. And she became excited and expressed how happy she was for me, and how sorry that she had not known about my birthday. So now, I had become 9 years old. All the other kids in that class had long since turned 9 years old.

ANOTHER MOVE

Anyway, the upshot of all this was, we soon moved again in mid March over to the next town, connected by a single road, to Corte Madera. And the public school in Corte Madera was called Neil Cummins school. I never learned who Neil Cummins was, but this was my third 4th grade class in the 1956-57 school year. It seems to me that as we moved from Mill Valley to Corte Madera, I tried out in March for the Mill Valley Little League. I think I did well in that tryout. Catching fly balls and grounders and because we had moved away from Mill Valley, I never took the batting phase tryout.

My last memory of the Mill Valley School was probably the day I left it for good. In Mill Valley, where we lived, we could not get any TV channels except one and the show I remember was "The Ray Milland Show" and playing Ray's wife was an actress I sort of formed a crush on: her name was Phyllis Avery. After leaving the Ray Milland Show, she appeared in the first season of the Perry Mason program, *"The Case of the Half-Awakened Wife."* I was shocked to learn that Phyllis Avery was not only the wife, but also the killer of her nasty husband. That Perry Mason show was the last I saw of Phyllis Avery.

. . .

But that last memory was instigated by the placement of our TV set in its new location: the garage of our new house located on 76 Mohawk Drive, Corte Madera, California. This was before zip codes, by the way. There I sat in front of our 1954 Silver-tone TV set, originally purchased from Sears Roebuck, and I found that in wide open Corte Madera, I could get all the TV channels that I was unable to receive in Mill Valley, backed up against that mountain. And, so I watched the "I Love Lucy" program for the first time, where the Ricardos lived out in the country and there were a bunch of baby chickens to take care of.

Anyway, the next day was probably my last day at the Mill Valley School, and I asked the nice girl who sat across from me if she had seen the I Love Lucy program the night before. Yes, she had! And she thought the program so funny and so wonderful. I felt an extra dimension of belonging that I had been unable to feel living in that non TV receptive house in Mill Valley.

But we had moved, so I went with my grandfather to sign up for Little League in Corte Madera. I remember I got assigned, although a somewhat late-comer to the Littleman's Grocery team. There were six teams in the Corte Madera Little League "Major League" category. I think that they had determined that I was not a part of the tryout team of Littleman's and unless I proved to be a sensation, I was penned in to join a minor league team. And so it came to be that I became a member of the Hornets Minor League team in the Corte Madera Little League. Our coach was a Mr. Ray Shunk. And I got assigned the 3rd base role. I think of all the grounders I fielded or didn't field, I threw out two runners all season long. But at least one of those runners I threw out at first base was in the championship game against the Bears. We won the game and the Minor League championship that year. Yeh Hornets!

I remember one Little League game I had to go pee. My mother was in her car watching and suffering as she noticed my suffering. I was manning my assigned 3rd base position. Pretty soon, I could not hold it any more and I wet my pants. And the pee streamed visibly down my blue jeans leg. The minor league teams supplied distinctly colored jerseys for each team; we didn't have real baseball uniforms. Our team, the Hornets, was supplied with yellow-body and black-sleeved jerseys, to identify us with the color of a hornet bee. All the kids wore blue jeans. And as there was no place to urinate around that baseball diamond, I peed into my pants.

SGT. PRESTON

But now I was in the school system, my third 4th grade class. My third 4th grade teacher of the 1956-57 school year was Mrs. Preston. Those were the three 4th grade teachers I had: Miss Prince, Mrs. Hildebrandt and Mrs. Preston. I think Mrs. Preston was a good teacher, though I was not with her long.

I think my first or second day in Mrs. Preston's class was picture day. That is, we were having our individual pictures taken. Probably because I was the new kid, I marched at the head of the boys line. I followed the last girl into the room they were going, and I heard screams all around me. As it happened, the girls went on mass into the girls' bathroom to look in mirrors, I guess, to make themselves presentable for the photographer. I had been unaware of this procedure, and had followed the girls into the girls' bathroom. Thus, I became a kind of instant pariah in the class. Of course, I left as soon as I could. I have no recollection of any photos being taken.

I read the Weekly Reader in class, we built "adobe model houses," learned about Father Junipero Serra and read about the Boston Marathon and John Kelly, who seemed to win the Boston Marathon each year in those days. One of my classmates was Amy Miller, whose father was a congressman who, while Amy and I were in Mrs. Preston's 4th grade class, was killed in a private plane crash.

One time, Mrs. Preston was kind of pissed with me because I had made a drawing of a naked woman producing a baby and I think I named it "Mrs. Preston." She did not like that much and sent me to sit outside the classroom, next to a fence which ran alongside the famous Corte Madera slough. This was where I met the first black kid I had ever been to school with. A kid named Harold had also been sent outside from a classroom a couple rooms up from mine. He smiled and waved at me, but that was it. I never saw him again.

. . .

Also in my class was Randi Natalini, Jackie McDermott, Bob Nelson and Andy Morse. I liked Randy. She was nuts about horses as I remember, and she was a pretty fast runner. I was kind of nuts about her, but I never dared to tell her that.

The fastest runner of all the kids in the 4th grade was a boy in another 4th grade class named Keith Taylor. Keith was a blonde haired kid, kind of small, popular with the girls, and in a foot race he could outrun anybody in the 4th grade. We also had softball challenges in the 4th grade. A school tradition that went right up to the highest grade in the school, the 8th grade. That was the grade where my sister Phoebe was attending. Her teacher was Mr. Veezy.

I would be remiss if I did not quote the song lyrics that they came up with in Mr. Veezy's class. (I am actually singing this as I am writing it.)

"Neil Cummins by the bubbling slough,
    Neil Cummins we love you, yes we do.
    So, fight, fight for Neil Cummins, fight 'til you're dead.
    And we will bury you at Neil Cummins with a math book on your head."

I BECOME THE STRIKEOUT KING

I thought I might become a real bonus to my class in the softball games. Mrs. Preston even announced that I had replaced Dana Christensen, a good hitter, who had lived at

76 Mohawk Drive and had now moved away. In the first game I remember, we were challenged by a 3rd grade class. I hit a home run, a measly sharp grounder "right down the third base line," as our team captain, Fred Ross, explained to someone.

But after that, I never seemed to hit anything. I became known as a strikeout king, a sure out. We played softball in those days in that particular town without baseball gloves. There was an art to playing the game bare handed. I was the new kid; I had to adjust to what they did. As for my failures at the plate, I don't know if a growth spurt caused my failure or what. But I could not hit the softball anywhere, until something happened in March 1958. But then I'm getting a bit ahead of myself.

That year, 1957, was the first time I saw Elgin Baylor playing basketball on TV. He played for Seattle University. I remember watching one game up in Inverness, California, near Half Moon Bay, where my grandfather was substituting as parish priest for that Sunday. We arrived in Inverness on Saturday afternoon, and that evening I remember watching California University playing Seattle University, live from Berkley, California.

Cal had a player named Earl Robinson. Years later, in 1965 to be exact, I remember being at a baseball game in Yankee Stadium where this same Earl Robinson, playing baseball for the Baltimore Orioles, hit a home run into the left field bleachers. But as for what Baylor did in that Cal game, I have no recollection of actually seeing him. I vaguely remember seeing Earl Robinson taking the ball out of bounds under one of the team's baskets.

PROMOTED

In the fall of 1957, I was promoted along with all the other kids to the fifth grade. My new teacher was a Mr. Kerr, who was, as I remember, a jolly sort, a terrible athlete, and a pretty good teacher. I noticed for the first time a healthy young girl named Janet Wieder. I was in love with this girl. Her best friend was a girl named Cindy.

In late 1957, we started to watch Perry Mason on TV. An hour program, near the end of which, Perry Mason always got the real killer to confess, in the courtroom during procedure, or outside of the courtroom. It seems to me that this show, starring Raymond Burr, came on every Saturday night at 7:30. On Friday nights, we watched the Dick Clark Beechnut gum show with guest appearances by such hit makers as Bobby Rydell and Richie Valens. The whole audience of teenage girls would sing the Beechnut Spearmint gum song. "It's flavorific!" I know my spell-checker will underline that word, but the song ended with that exact term. "Beechnut gum is keen, it's wrapped in green, ...it's flavorific!" sang the audience each week.

HALLOWEEN - I GO AS THE BABE

For Halloween that year, I dressed up as Babe Ruth. I had seen pictures of Ruth in his latter day Yankees road uniform, and my mother and my sister, Phoebe, did their best to make a shirt for me, with the logo "New York" on the front, and the number "3" on the back. Plus, I put a small pillow in my shirt to make it appear that I had a big belly, a La Ruth at that time.

My mother's best friends from her days in the Episcopal church in San Francisco, were the Hensleys, Guy and Corrine. They were good friends, and they were also bridge, the card game, enthusiasts. Bridge became the basis for get-togethers. A week-end rarely went by without a visit from or to the Hensleys.

GUY AND CORRINE

Corrine was a jolly fat woman, who had no sense of smell. As she had no sense of smell, she often smelled bad. Her odor was memorable. She was from New Orleans, and had attended the University of Oklahoma. A mathematics wizard who worked for Merrill Lynch in San Francisco, she earned a pretty nice income from her job. She was married to Guy Hensley.

Guy Hensley was a homosexual. He privately told my mother that he had never touched Corrine. He told her of some of his trysts, for example, with a soldier with "broad shoulders" in a motel room. Guy worked as a fund-raiser, a job for which he drove all over the country, and apparently resulted in some sexual triumphs along the way. My mother told me to be careful around Guy.

· · ·

I remember one day during a bridge game in Corte Madera, Guy Hensley was apparently "the dummy" for one hand, and he demonstrated for me why Hitler had trained his troops to do the goose step. And then Guy proceeded to goose step around the living room, saying how the goose step strengthened the calf muscles of the leg.

NOTRE DAME ENDS OKLAHOMA'S WINNING STREAK

That fall of 1957, I was in the Hensley's San Francisco apartment. My mother had joined the Hensleys for some function or other, leaving me alone in their apartment. They had a modern new television and I turned on the TV to watch a football game from Norman, Oklahoma; Notre Dame vs. the University of Oklahoma. Oklahoma at the time was undefeated going back years to the point where I believe they had won 47 straight games. The Hensleys were rabid Oklahoma fans.

What I do remember was rooting hard for Notre Dame to win the game. Notre Dame had Nick Pietrosante as their fullback and George Izzo as their quarterback. I remember Izzo could throw hard spiral passes but I think his completion rate was rather low. Pietrosante was magnificent. And in the end, Notre Dame, coached by Terry Brennan, upset Oklahoma, coached by Bud Wilkerson, 7-0.

I believe 1957 was the year I lost my bicycle. The bike was way too big for me. When I sat on the seat, my feet could not reach the pedals. There were no gears on it — a straight forward pedal bicycle. My grandfather had bought the bike for me the year before. He probably got a great deal on it, but it was really too big for me. When I reported it missing, my grandfather became angry and told me to go find it. I did find the bicycle left on the playground of the Neil Cummins School, and brought it back home, walking the bike, as I still could not reach the pedals.

At Christmas in December 1957, still an 8 year-old, I was determined to catch Santa Claus as he came into our living room. I waited up in the dark of the living room. I don't remember if we had a fire place at that time, but I do remember we had a tree. As it happened, I think I must have gone off to bed, and was unable to catch Santa doing anything.

We had our usual Christmas breakfast the next morning with pig sausages and country gravy.

CHAPTER 8

CORTE MADERA, CALIFORNIA – STILL IN MARIN COUNTY

———

THE HEADLINES **in 1958**

- Jan 1 European Economic Community, better known as the European Common Market starts operation
- Mar 27 Nikita Khrushchev becomes Soviet Premier as well as First Secretary of the Communist Part
- May 23 Mao Zedong starts the "Great Leap Forward" movement in China
- Sep 12 US Supreme Court orders the all-white Central High School in Little Rock, Arkansas to integrate
- Dec 19 1st radio broadcast from space, US President Dwight D. Eisenhower Christmas message "to all mankind, America's wish for peace on Earth and goodwill to men everywhere"

- Dec 31 Cuban dictator Fulgencio Batista tells his Cabinet he is fleeing the country[1]

January 18, 1958, was the day of my 10th birthday. I have to say, this is one of the most memorable birthdays I have ever had. My mother had arranged a little birthday party for me. Seated at the dining room table were my neighborhood friends, 12 year-old Ken Goodreau, 11 year-old Jackie Peetz and his younger brother, 9 year-old Ronnie Peetz. These guys were my best friends at the time. We had lived in this house at 76 Mohawk Drive, in Corte Madera, California for nearly one year.

KEN GOODREAU

I did not know Ken Goodreau well at the time. But I felt I had to invite the big guy, and he was outsized big. His mom was a registered nurse, the sole breadwinner of the house, and she was noticeably cock-eyed. But Ken was the life of the party. He told us what he called a dirty joke. I may have been a little fearful of what he was going to say, but as it turned out, his dirty joke was "The white horse fell in the mud!" That was his dirty joke. I think we all laughed at that one.

The four of us boys had a nice birthday dinner. I do not recall anyone gave me any presents at the time, but after-wards, we retired to the garage-turned-rec room and turned off all the lights. I think we had some empty cardboard boxes in the room, and we began throwing these boxes at each other. Tremendous fun, as I recall, but midway, a couple of times, Ronnie Peetz got clobbered and started to cry. Both times this happened, we turned on the lights and consoled Ronnie until he stopped crying. Then we turned off the lights and resumed playing. Ronnie was a good sport.

RICKY NELSON CAN SING!

This was also the year that my sister, Phoebe, came running out of her bedroom shouting, "Phil, Ricky Nelson can sing!" This was a revelation to me and I guess to America, for we had originally accustomed ourselves to watching the Nelsons, and seeing Little Ricky as the proverbial little kid clown of the show. He always got laughs. Except for the most recent Nelson programs, over the past couple of years. Ricky had grown into a teenager and had become quiet and somewhat of a spare tire in my estimation.

Now, he had recorded records and like his mom twenty years before him, become a singing star. Probably he exceeded what his mom had ever done. With the support of singing appearances on the show, he had become an international super star. We now watched the Nelsons and Ricky singing such hits as "Bee-bop Baby" and "Poor Little Fool." The TV show made it possible for the kid to shine. He started to rival Elvis.

WET PANTS

In late February 1958, I did something rather thoughtless and for which I have little or no explanation. Sitting in Mr. Kerr's 5th grade class, during a session focused on arithmetic, I kind of had to pee. And, as I remember, I decided on making some sort of experiment. I peed a little into my pants. And then, to further the experiment, I took paper and tried to dry my crotch area. Then I made the mistake of telling one or two of the kids in my class—probably Andy Morse and his buddy John Warren—of the experiment. Big mistake, as this revelation on my part led to a rather unexpected commotion.

After school, I remember walking home on Mohawk Drive. A group of kids, led by Fred Ross, who was now a member of a different 5th grade class from me—he belonged to Mr. Zaro's class—now confronted me. "Hey Pallett." (I still spelled my name without the "e" on the end). "We hear you wet your pants."

"No, I didn't," I protested. "I was experimenting." They wanted to see, and whatever test they made to make their conclusion, I do not remember. "Yeah, they're wet," stated Fred Ross. The other kids laughed, and we went our separate ways.

The next week, March 1958, Mr. Zaro's class in the persons of Tom Gootherts and Keith Taylor, came into our class and challenged us to a softball match. This was a common occurrence in those days. Again, I reiterate, we played softball bare-handed without gloves.

REVENGE LIKE NEVER BEFORE

The game took place March 4, 1958, a bright sunny day in Corte Madera, California. Keith Taylor was pitching for Mr. Zaro's class. I remember I came up and the kids from Zaro's class started chanting "Hey, Pallett. You gonna wet your pants?" They kept saying this, and kept saying this. Meanwhile, I stood at the plate thinking how unfair this was. After all, it had been an experiment I was trying.

Keith Taylor, a left-hander, underhanded the pitch to me, and I slammed the ball way over the left fielder's head. I headed around the bases for a home run. The next time I came up, they were all quiet. Taylor pitched me the ball and I again slammed a ball, not so high this time, but a line drive hard to the opposite field. The right fielder had no chance, and I again rounded the bases for a home run.

I have never forgotten this date. March 4, 1958. And I remember writing on the bottom of the sole of my bedroom slipper, "March 4, 1958. I hit 2 home runs in a softball game." I believe Fred Ross was in the field that day. He never mentioned my having wet my pants again. No one ever did. And from then on, I belonged to a group of guys who could hit.

Besides the Hensleys, my mother also had friends from San Francisco, the Mitchells, whom I mentioned briefly before, Ken and Gladys. Kenneth Mitchell was a diminutive man, small in stature but big on guts. He was a hemophiliac, who, during World War II, had joined a Scottish commando unit. He fought in the Middle East against Rommel's German forces, and when once wounded, nearly bled to death.

Although my grandfather and I played catch in the back yard in Corte Madera, Kenneth played soccer and though we did not have a ball with which to demonstrate, Kenneth told us that to kick a ball properly in soccer, you had to use the side of your foot. Ken also sold insurance. That was his bread winning job. Ken and Gladys had three kids. One was Janet, Ken's daughter from an earlier marriage, and she was what was called in those days, retarded. Gladys, his beautiful wife, was from the state of Oregon. That was all I knew of her at that time.

PHILIP WETS THE BED!

I remember from this time how my sister Phoebe put her head outside her bedroom window and shouted out to the street, "Philip wets the bed! Philip wets the bed!" Of course, I was terribly embarrassed by this. But not long afterwards, Ken Goodreau came up with a nickname for Phoebe. He called her "Fleabite." I seemed to feel this terribly bothered my sister, being called Fleabite all the time by Ken Goodreau. I can still hear him call her. "Hey, Fleabite!"

We also had a girl in the neighborhood who lived at the first house on our block, in a house right across from Ken Goodreau's house. Her name was Jean, and I do not remember her last name. But she was the same age as Ken Goodreau, a good-looking girl, but her main claim to fame back then was that she was a terrific softball player. I think she was in the 7th grade at the time, and we always thought that she and Ken should be boyfriend and girlfriend. Ken, I think supported the idea, but I don't think Jean was so hot about it.

PHILLIP RILEY

One incident sticks out from the spring of 1958. We had in our class a kid named Phillip Riley, who was not a good student; he was also an epileptic, who from time to time would have epileptic fits in the classroom. We would all move our desks apart and let Phillip, laying on the ground, have his epileptic fit. Soon he would return to normal, and class would resume. I remember Phillip as being a pretty fast runner, faster than me, but he was not a good athlete.

This one day, I think Phillip had asked to be excused to go to the bathroom. And for some reason, I decided I would surreptitiously go to the bathroom as well, to query him, to bug him a little about getting special treatment from Mr. Kerr. And so, I remember asking Mr. Kerr if I could go to the bathroom. He assented and I went to the bathroom, and started to bug Phillip Riley with some questions, like what was so special about his relationship to Mr. Kerr. I did not get far. Mr. Kerr stormed into the bathroom, grabbed me, shook me, and demanded to know what business I had in there to question Phillip about anything. This is all I remember, except I probably apologized to Phillip and the incident was forgotten.

MAJOR LEAGUER

Well, that spring, I soon joined a major league Little League team for the first time. I proudly received and wore the uniform, white with red piping, of Koch Fiberglass, the uniform bearing the number 5. The Koch company, which made luggage out of fiberglass, was one of six organizations which sponsored Little League teams. There were also Bowman Electric, color green, North Bay Lumber, color yellow, South Bay Lumber, color black, the Lions Club, color gold and Littleman's Supermarket, color blue. Six teams in all. The league still played on a baseball diamond outside on the grounds of Neil Cummins Elementary School. There was no grass on the field, simply dirt.

This is me in my Koch Fibreglass uniform. Corte Madera, California 1958 as photographed by Marty Allison.

I did not play much, and when I did, I struck out about every time. Hitting a pitched baseball was not the same as hitting a pitched softball. The pitchers in the Twin Cities

Little League at the time all pitched overhand, like their adult brethren. And I swung and missed a bit.

I remember one game I had to hit against Mike Telligence, who was a big hard-throwing left hander, the best in the league, whom almost no one hit. Big Jim Troppmann, his battery mate, was the catcher. I struck out on three pitches. Meanwhile, Bill Ayres, a kid in my class at school, though older than I was, came up batting left handed and determined to hit the ball.

Even though he was at a disadvantage, batting left-handed against a big, hard-throwing left hander, Bill determinedly swung and hit a hard ground ball that went past the second baseman for a hit. This was something I never forgot. I had to admire Bill, who was somewhat known for his toughness, but poor performance in the classroom. Bill was the boyfriend of Jackie McDermott, who was a good-looking, though overweight girl in our class.

In this year, I actually did see Elgin Baylor playing on TV. He played for the Minneapolis Lakers, and in the game I remember, he scored 55 points. He played against the Detroit Pistons, with Gene Shue. Other shows I watched on TV included The Steve Allen Show on NBC We much preferred this program to the Ed Sullivan

Me in Koch Fibreglass uniform, Corte Madera, California - 1958 Again the photo credit belongs to Marty Allison.

Show, which aired on CBS, and which it seemed most of America watched.

Steve Allen did crazy stuff. Like the night he had Jerry lee Lewis playing Great Balls Afire. Jerry Lee was pounding away at the piano, stood up and the piano bench slid out of the TV view behind him. While Jerry Lee continued to pound out the music, the bench came flying back across the screen. You knew that off camera, Steve Allen had caught the bench and had thrown it back. Steve also had the Men on the Street. Louie Nye, Tom Poston, and Don Knotts; these three guys were hilarious. I wouldn't miss them for anything.

PROMOTED

After that summer of 1958, we 5th graders were promoted into the 6th grade, and I joined Mr. Johnson's class. I was happy to see that Janet Wieder was still in my class, as were John Warren, Andy Morse, Tommy Gootherts, Ricky Cuff and Keith Taylor. We even had a new guy in our class: Michael Stiltner. Michael was a kid from an economically poor family. His sneakers, that he always wore, had holes in them. He wore old hand-me-down clothes, and he was kind of rough and well-muscled.

TEARS ON MY PILLOW, PAIN IN MY HEART

Michael Stiltner, it so happened, took a great liking to Janet Wieder, which made me somewhat jealous, and one day, he got up and sang the song by Little Anthony and the Imperials, "Tears on my Pillow." That was Michael's contribution to Show and Tell and I think he sang it directly to Janet.

Meanwhile, that summer, my grandmother had had enough of California. Even though my mother and grandfather had created a special brickwork bordering our new patio in Corte Madera, a brickwork which contained soil for plants that my grandmother could tend to, she could not stand living in what she felt was an isolated living circumstance. And so, my grandfather purchased a house in Seattle proper, and my grandparents moved there.

I was a talkative fellow, myself. I remember for Show and Tell, a regular activity in our school year, I would get up and tell everyone what happened that week-end. I began each Show and Tell session with, "Well, Saturday, when we went up to Inverness..." Whatever I said after that, to this day, I have no recollection. I also won a spelling bee about that time. I recall my final two opponents were a cute girl named Christie, and Keith Taylor. I don't remember how Christie got eliminated, but the teacher gave Keith Taylor the word "Quebec" to spell. I think Keith started it out with a "C" instead of a "Q". The result was that I spelled it, and won the spelling bee.

FRANKENSTEIN

For Halloween that year, I dressed up as Frankenstein's monster. My sister and my mother went all out this time. I remember they taped these little protrusions on the sides of my neck to show the electrodes that the monster had. They provided an old sports jacket for me to wear, and they went to town making up my face to look like Boris Karloff as the monster. I remember going through the neighborhood knocking on all the doors to get candy, but I created screams from the little girls also going Trick-or-Treating in the neighborhood as I, with arms raised, followed them.

I was trying to impress Mr. Johnson with my ability in sports. In one intramural football game, the class star athlete, Tom Gootherts, was quarterbacking. He was always good. This one time, his team was close to the goal line. I was playing against him, He went back to pass and I could read his thought process. He was going to pass to his right to Keith Taylor who would cross the goal line. As he reared back to throw the pass, I started in the opposite direction. I guess today, we would call it jumping the route. Anyway, that is what I did; he passed the ball and on the run I intercepted it against my chest and ran the other way for a touchdown. I thought that would impress Mr. Johnson, but apparently it did not.

My mother rode the bus each day into San Francisco, about 14 miles away. The Greyhound bus company supplied the buses. My mother worked at the time for Jofa, a fabrics company with headquarters in Chicago. They supplied fabrics for all kinds of furniture and curtains. She sometimes mentioned her fat, lazy co-worker named Richard. And she also mentioned her boss in Chicago, Mr. Timmerman.

MY MOM'S ROMANCE

About this time, in 1958, my mother became familiar with her bus driver, who turned out to be Kenneth Buetner. I remember my grandmother telling me that it would be a good idea if my mother married Mr. Buetner. "Then you could take his name," my grandmother told me. One day I went to the playground with Kenneth Buetner, and we shot baskets. His style of shooting was rather old fashioned, as he did not shoot a jump shot, which was then, all the rage.

One day, Kenneth Buetner brought me an electric train set that we set up on a large plywood board in the rec room, where the old piano and the TV existed. Then my mother and Ken Buetner sat together kissing and necking on the couch while I played with the train set. I kept wrecking the train, which interrupted the love scene three or four times. I think I was in a playful mood, for pretty soon, I dropped a large flashlight battery down my mother's dress in the back. And Kenneth dutifully dropped his hand down my mother's dress to retrieve the battery. This happened a couple of times. Kenneth was reluctant to be strict with me in any sense. I finally left them alone.

My grandparents moving away placed an added burden on my mother to make the mortgage payments on the house in Corte Madera. Although my grandfather and Marty had pledged to help her, Marty had now moved into a separate living quarters also in Corte Madera, but she no longer contributed to the mortgage payments. And my grandfather now had to make payments on the house in Seattle, leaving my mother as the sole financier of the Corte Madera house.

The year 1959 was about to come upon us. This was a year that started out with such promise for me, but terminated in such sadness and deprivation. End of story. The years 1959 to my move east in 1964 will be the subject of the next section of my little book.

CHAPTER 9

PHOENIX, ARIZONA – LITTLE LEAGUE LOST

———

THE HEADLINES **in 1959**

- Fidel Castro comes to power in Cuba after Revolution.
- United States Vice President Richard Nixon and the Soviet Union's Premier Nikita Khrushchev engage in an impromptu debate.
- The Dalai Lama and tens of thousands of Tibetans flee to India after China Invades Tibet.[1]

By 1959, Kenneth was proposing marriage to my mother. She seemed willing, as Kenneth could assume the payments on the house in Corte Madera, relieving my mother of some pressure. My grandmother thought it a great idea, because I could take his name and be Philip Buetner.

· · ·

One Saturday our mother gathered Phoebe and me together and asked us point-blank if we approved of her marrying Kenneth Buetner. Both my sister and I were against the marriage, and we emphatically said so. Thereupon, our mother picked up the phone on the wall in the kitchen and called Kenneth. "Ken," she said, "the kids don't want it."

THE BIG SWITCH

And that was that. Kenneth wanted me to keep the train set he had given me. I remember he came to the house, subdued but friendly, to pick up a new television set he had apparently given us for our living room. He picked up the set and left and I never heard of nor saw him again.

On February 3, in a snowy field in Iowa, Buddy Holly died. I remember the San Francisco radio stations played mournful tributes. We knew of Buddy Holly records, and also being killed on that plane were Ritchie Valens and the Big Bopper. The latter two guys I remember seeing perform on TV. Valens was 17. I was unaware that Ritchie Valens was also a Spanish-speaking rock star and I had not heard of "La Bamba" at the time. We knew him for his hit "Donna."

All along this time my mother had related stories of an interior decorator who ordered fabrics from Jofa, a Mr. Ortega. She kept mentioning Mr. Ortega, and then one day, we met Mr. Ortega. Soon my mother and Mr. Ortega were dating. It turned out that Mr. Ortega was of Mexican origin, who claimed that his family had at one time owned "half of the land in Mexico." Ortega played bridge well enough to play with my mother and the Henleys.

Pretty soon Ortega was staying overnight in our house, in my mother's bedroom. One night he and my mother went out, and they left me alone to have my dinner in Bob's Restaurant in the Corte Madera mall. Actually, I thought that was kind of cool. I think I ordered hamburger with no bun. I was all by myself. And from there I must have walked home.

Ortega gathered my sister and me together, along with my mother, and asked us if we had any objection to his marrying my mother. I remember I stated that as long as I could stay and play Little League baseball for Koch Fiberglass, I had no objection. But that was my principal concern and, you might call it, my stipulation. I was rather adamant about this requisite at the time. Baseball meant everything to me.

This, even though I had earlier somewhat of an epiphany playing in a basketball game. Our team was coached by Mr. Zaro, who had been a 5th grade teacher, and was now a 6th grade teacher. He had the reputation of being knowledgeable about sports. And, as it turned out, he was a pretty nice guy. During this particular after school basketball game, played with a kick ball, or soccer ball, rather than a non available basketball, I scored 14 points.

· · ·

And in one moment, I, for some reason got fed up with what was happening on the court, and from the head of the key on our offensive side of the court, with my back to the basket, I bounced the ball once and shot a hook shot from this tremendous distance. The shot went in and practically stopped the game, so shocking a moment. To see somebody shoot from that distance with such an unlikely hook shot was not done.

After the game, I don't remember if we won or lost, we were gathered together and I remember Mr. Zaro in particular looking at me and saying, "You have a fine center." I guess I was playing center, but what I knew about basketball at the time was little. I guess Mr. Zaro had told my teacher, Mr. Johnson, about the shot. And I remember Mr. Johnson saying he was going to work with me on my hook shot. He never did.

WRESTLEMANIA

We used to get into fights in those days. Wrestling matches. Punching someone was somewhat taboo. My first and foremast opponent was a kid named Geoff Hewlett. I don't know why to this day, but for some reason, Geoff Hewlett did not like me, and I disliked Geoff Hewlett. We wrestled two or three times. One time, Mr. Zaro came and broke us up. He banged our heads together, and I think he made us shake hands.

I did battle with Tom Parispolo, who was reputed to be the strongest kid ounce for ounce of my classmates. And sure enough, Tom beat me in wrestling. No one fooled with Tom Parispolo. Then there was Mike Thomas. I don't remember how I got into it with him, but I think he kept hassling me to the point where I agreed to fight him. As I got on top of him, about to claim victory, he kept saying that he was a proud Portugue. I ground his knuckles against the asphalt, and he kept saying he was a proud Portugue. I took it to mean that he was Portuguese descent, and he was proud of that.

I got around to challenging Andy Morse to a fight. Andy was one of the most popular guys in our school, let alone our class. He had been my classmate since the 4th grade, and he was best friends with our baseball catcher, John Warren. Andy was not a great athlete, but he had finished winning a tough wrestling match with Tom Gootherts, who was probably the best athlete and unassailably the toughest guy we had in our class. Andy got Tom down and pinned him. I remember Tom saying the next time he fought with Andy, there would be no wrestling, there would be punching and Tom meant to punch Andy out.

Well, I knew Andy was tough and strong, as he had beaten everybody. When I started to provoke him in a sandbox, as I remember, he was reluctant to battle with me. Sure, he was nearly a year older than I was, and he was strong. But I persisted. We went at it, and he beat me fair and square in wrestling.

That spring, we played the 6th grade softball championship between the two 6th grade classes on the best baseball diamond they had at Neil Cummins School, Mr. Zaro's class against Mr. Johnson class. We, the Johnsons, were ahead 5-2 in the final inning. They had last ups, and I was playing second base. We had one out, but they had a runner on 3rd base. The batter hit a ball on the ground directly at me.

As I mentioned, we played softball without gloves. I caught the ground ball while the runner was advancing from 3rd base to home. Out teacher, Mr. Johnson, yelled at me to throw home and get the runner. But I knew baseball, better than he did. Taking the sure out, I tossed the ball to the 1st baseman for the putout and let the runner score. This made the score 5-3, bases now empty and two outs. This was the best decision to make, rather than risk not getting the runner at home and allowing the batter to reach 1st base or even 2nd base, and there would still be 1 out.

The other team was coached by their teacher, Mr. Zaro, who knew baseball way better than our Mr. Johnson. But I would have to say on the whole, Mr. Johnson was a pretty good guy. He played the guitar and he sang. He was a nice person. And Mr. Johnson's class won the Championship over Mr. Zaro's class, 5-3.

We discovered a new sprint champion in 1959. At first, we had this new kid, and he was in Mr. Zaro's class. His name was Jim Franzi, and he was a damn good athlete, a fast runner, and a good-looking kid, as well. But the sprinting champion, better than Franzi, was a kid named Buzzy

Salata. Buzz had remained not one of the "in crowd" at the school in all my time there. I think he was in the 4th and 5th grades with me. But he emerged with his sprinting prowess in the 6th grade. People noticed him.

During a PTA meeting, my mother went to the school and met with Mr. Johnson. "Don't tell him that!" This I remember her telling me what Mr. Johnson said when my mother said something about me to him.

MY BEST FRIEND

Also, around this time, my best friend had become David Berner. David lived on Mohawk Drive, three or so houses up from ours. His family was rather strict and at first, David was not allowed to play with us other kids like Ken Goodreau and Jackie Peetz. I think David's family members were strict church goers. David's younger sister was called Missy, perhaps Ruth was her actual name. I am not sure. I remember her as Missy. I will say that David and I became close friends, and we played a lot of baseball together.

At first, Mr. Berner seemed reluctant to warm up to me, nor to entertain his son's enthusiasm for me as a friend. I can remember one incident in their garage, and I don't remember what was going on but Mr. Berner lit into me for whatever I was doing. Then I told David that I had shaved my forearm. I think David told his dad, and they both got the impression I was pretty weird.

· · ·

Another time, Mr. Berner took David and me to a baseball game at Seals Stadium between the Milwaukee Braves and the San Francisco Giants. We were out in the right field bleacher area, and I remember seeing Hank Aaron's number 44 near to me. At one point, the Giants made a substitution, putting in Eddie Bressoud to play either short-stop or second base.

I remember Mr. Berner looking at the player's number and checking his program. "That's Bresowd," he said, mispro-nouncing a name that I knew well from listening the past year and a half to the Giants broadcasts. "Bras-SUE," I corrected him. "That's Eddie Bressoud," and I remember Mr. Berner did not reply to my correction. He nodded his head.

I actually coached David with everything I knew about baseball. He seemed to like me and enjoyed my coaching him. We became best friends. And when it came time for Little League to start up in the spring of 1959, Mr. Berner — and I have no way of verifying this — but, I believe he somehow coerced the Little League officials to put David with my team at Koch Fiberglass. Even though I had turned 11 years old, I was slated to be a major part of the Koch team that spring.

JOHN PAUL JONES?

In the meantime, Al Ortega married my mother. Ortega bragged that he had been in the United States Navy during

World War 2 and had won more citations than anyone in the US Navy since John Paul Jones.

During Little League, our first game was against South Bay Lumber on a Saturday afternoon, and they had a veteran pitcher whose first name was Jack, and his last name was something like Bagliotta. He threw left-handed and I did not think he was that difficult to hit. The first time I came up against him, I lined a base hit to center to the right of the 2nd base bag.

I had adopted the hitting style I had seen on television of Gino Cimoli. Cimoli had his feet together and stepped into the pitch. I had determined that this aspect of hitting, the stepping into the pitch, was the most important thing I could do to get my weight into the pitch, and using my whole body to drive the pitch.

I used this approach against Bagliotta and it seemed to work. I came up against him again and lined a pitch to center. I distinctly remember coming up against him a third time with the bases loaded. He looked at me and turned away, and blew air out between his lips, looking exasperated as if to say, "Oh, no. Not this guy again." He pitched and I got a third hit. I swung hard and managed to hit the ball off the end of the bat and the ball spun off into right field for a clean single. A run scored.

. . .

Somehow, the rest of my teammates did not fare so well against Jack Bagliotta, for we lost the game 10-2.

Games later, I came up against Jack Bagliotta again and hit a long drive that took one bounce over the fence for a ground rule double. I remember the first basemen commenting "Nice hit," as I rounded first base and headed into 2nd base.

But perhaps the most memorable game I played in was one where I did not start. Art Marshall, our manager, put me into right field in the 5th inning. Little League games were limited to 6 innings in those days. We were behind 5-4 and Steve Marshall, the coach's son, was pitching for us. For our opponent, pitching was Al Weckel, a big, powerful left-hander who I judged was tougher to hit than Jack Bagliotta because he threw so hard.

A PSYCHO-CYBERNETIC MOMENT

In the last inning, the bottom of the 6th, I came up. As I mentioned, we were down 5-4, and my mother and step-father, Al Ortega were in the crowd watching the game. I used my new batting stance. A good friend of mine named Barry, a red-headed guy, played 3rd base for Bowman Elec-tric. I remember being determined against Weckel. I gripped the bat hard, which was perhaps not the best idea to hit naturally against a tough pitcher. But I gripped the bat, and when the pitch came, I stepped into it.

. . .

The bases were empty, no outs. I slammed Weckel's hard pitch on a line drive, to the right of the 2nd baseman and a hit that went all the way to the wall in center field. I rounded 1st and headed towards 2nd. I went in standing up as the throw came in. I remember a rather desperate-sounding Al Weckel shouting "Get him!" to his infielder, whoever caught the ball from the outfielder. They tagged me, but I was already standing on the base, safe.

After that, Kevin Wilson, one of our young stars, came up. He was perhaps inspired by my hit, but in any event, he hit the ball into the outfield. I raised my head and tried to see, but I could see nothing. I changed my view to focus on our the 3rd base coach, and he was signaling me to run to 3rd base, which meant that the ball was not caught in the outfield. I ran to 3rd and the coach kept signaling me to run home. I scored the tying run and the score was now 5-5 with Steve Marshall, the coach's son coming up.

I don't remember what the hit was, but Steve got a hit and drove Kevin Wilson home with the winning run. I was pleased to be an integral part of the win, getting it started, so to speak. I was proud to be seen by my mother and step-father. Little did I know at the time that this would be the next to last game I would ever play in Little League, and my last hit.

FINAL GAME

I remember the next game I played was on Saturday against North Bay Lumber. Dick Newberry was pitching, and I was determined to get a hit. As it happened I stepped into one of Newberry's deliveries, perhaps a bit too soon, for I hit the ball squarely, but nearly straight up.

The kid in left field was Richard Kerns. I remember thinking he was not a good player. But he settled under my high pop fly. The ball probably would have hit him on the head if he didn't catch it, but he caught it. And that was the final plate appearance of my Little League career.

We moved out of 76 Mohawk Drive the next day. My mother told me in earnest that she would not have been able to keep up the mortgage payments. Grandpa was supposed to help. That was the original plan, but Grandpa was no longer in the picture. Now we moved into a rented house about 75 miles south of the city of San Francisco. I thought I would be able to continue my Little League appearances, but alas, this was beyond reality. After the season, a belea-guered Coach Marshall called our house and demanded I return the Koch uniform. Otherwise, he said, he would have to pay for the uniform. And so, with considerable sadness, I packed up the uniform and mailed it back to Mr. Marshall.

I remember a lot from that summer. One day, my step-father made me hoe up the entire front garden to make it ready for planting. I remember while out there listening to a San Francisco Giants baseball game. Two rookies had been up from Phoenix, Willie McCovey and Jose Pagan. I, along with the Giants broadcasters, Russ Hodges and Lon Simmons, were delighted with the fact that whatever team the Giants were playing could not get Willie McCovey out. He got three straight line drive singles, thus proving that his outstanding performance in Phoenix earlier that year had been no fluke. Welcome to the major leagues, Mr. McCovey!

Also in that house, I remember we played Canasta with three decks of cards, the game having been taught to us by Al Ortega. One afternoon, Phoebe received a visit from one of her friends, Amorette Nelson. Amorette was a rather pretty girl of 16 or so. I had discovered in the garage of that old house a collection of 78 records. Among these records was a recording of "Smoke Gets In Your Eyes," recorded by Benny Goodman and Helen Forrest around 1940. I played it over and over, and I played it for Amorette. She wanted to know if the lyrics said: "they asked me how I knew, my true love was true!" Amorette could not decide if the last word was "true" or "through." I wondered myself, so I could not tell her definitively.

BY THE TIME I GOT TO PHOENIX

Late that summer, we ended up in a motel in Phoenix, Arizona. Oh, it was so hot. I had no idea what was going on professionally with Al Ortega. Wasn't he an interior decorator? Didn't he have a practice in the San Francisco area? Well, in the meantime, my sister and I spent time in that motel pool. I did not know how to swim. I was 11 years old at the time, and my playmate was a 9 year-old kid, who tried in shallow water to play with me.

· · ·

He said to lay down on the bottom of the pool, holding my breath, of course, and then open my eyes and try to wave to him. In 3 feet of water. I did what he asked. At least, I tried to do as he asked. Much to my amazement, I was unable to lay on the bottom of the pool in 3 feet of water. Instead, I was floating. Floating? Me? I can't swim! But here I was, floating! From then on, I tried holding my breath and kicking and stroking all over that damned little pool, even the deep end. For the first time in my life, I was actually swimming.

Well, I never forgot that a 9 year-old kid "taught" me how to swim in a motel pool. I was also fascinated by the fact that in Phoenix, Arizona, we could pick up the Los Angeles Dodgers baseball games on radio. I could actually listen in to hear Duke Snider playing! On top of that, because Phoenix was the San Francisco Giants Triple AAA team in the minor leagues, the Giants had arranged for the Giants games to be broadcast in Phoenix!

I think my new step-father, Al Ortega, did try to make a life. He never beat me, ever. Supposedly, I found out later, he did propose running away with my 16 year-old sister, Phoebe. Well, she was my half-sister, as I later realized. Al often cooked us breakfast; horrible pancakes he made for us. He was often seen wandering around the house naked from the waist up.

He did take me once to a Phoenix Giants baseball game, which for me was a somewhat sorrowful experience. We now lived in a half of a duplex building at 29 Encanto Drive, right in the city of Phoenix. Mr. and Mrs. Waidner, the owners of the dwelling, lived in the other half of the duplex. I think they had a granddaughter who lived with them named Edie Waidner. She went to the West Phoenix High School with my sister.

KENILWORTH

I started out in school, now the 7th grade, in the Kenilworth School. Mr. Tamarin was our physical education teacher, and Mrs. Schweitzer was our home room teacher and general everything teacher. There were four 7th grade classes. My class was the 7-1s. We had an art teacher, Mrs. Parker whose written assessment of me on my report card was: "Talks.", and we had a shop teacher whose name escapes me. I think we went to those classes twice a week. The thing I remember is that in those classes, the art and the shop classes, I made tangible pieces of art that I have until this day, more than 60 years later. From no other school do I have anything from the time I spent there. I still find this noteworthy.

We had white kids in the school during 1959-1960. I remember talking with a nice girl named Susan in my Art and Home room classes. Her best friend was Cecilia, who was of Hispanic North American Indian descent, and had such a nice sweet personality. I remember she once suffered a needle going through her finger in the Home Economics class the girls had to take, while the boys were in the Shop class. There were a Mexican Indians attending the school, but no black kids. We had school dances, and I remember that I had a crush on the prettiest girl in the 7th grade. She was in the 7-2s and her name was Penny Craig. I think, as I remember, she liked me for a day and a half. But then she dropped me like a hot potato.

PENNY CRAIG

I later learned that she attended the Episcopal church that I could have attended, but never did; the Episcopal cathedral of Phoenix. If I had known she was there, I might have developed a friendship with her. But this did not happen at the time. Nor was it ever to happen.

Our family became addicted to television watching in those days. Perry Mason had become a real hit, and we also watched Rawhide. Phoebe attended high school. And I was at football practice. We played flag football and Coach Tamarin put me on the line, playing offensive tackle. We were in a single wing formation.

I remember 38 was our main play, where the quarterback would run the ball behind blocking to the right side. One other play we were practicing was a pass play where Roberto, our quarterback, took the ball and went back to pass. I tried to block this big kid from the 8th grade named Tony. He pancaked me, and knocked me hard at my throat. Play stopped while coach and all the other players gathered around me. I was okay and got up.

. . .

But in those days, I was plagued by bad colds which would take me four days to get over. The first bad cold I got during the football season kept me home, and when I got back to school, i did not return to football practice. I remember the class football games. Once we were playing at lunch and in one scramble for a loose ball, I was on the ground and somebody kicked me hard in the back. I was in such pain, I ended up in the nurse's office, but the pain went away and I returned to class.

In the early days of my school year in Phoenix, I was paired with Bobby Phillips, who was known as a talented downfield passer. In our Physical Education classes, Phillips soon discovered that I could catch his far downfield flings, get behind the defense and catch a pass on the run. One day, while I was still on the football team, the young guys on the team were separated for a game with another school. I was of course on the team with Phillips. He wanted me to play one of the backfield positions so that I could run downfield and catch one of his passes. But I yelled out "I don't know the plays!" I meant that I didn't know the scripted responsibilities for that particular position. And, so I did not play that position, and missed a chance to catch a ball from Phillips in a real game.

Soon after, Bobby Phillips moved away. I saw him one more time when he visited one of our Saturday night school dances. I was wearing a straw hat, trying to look cool. I remember I must have left the hat on my chair, which Bobby Phillips was now occupying. He good naturedly tossed the hat to me, sort of like old times. And I dropped it.

FOOTBALL CAPTAIN

For some reason, the boys in my class made me captain of the 7-1 football team. Midway, Danny Reid, the muscular kid who was in our class, told me he would not play because he had to save himself for the school's football team. Danny played for us. We had some pretty good guys, and I was surprised they chose me over Danny, Jim (tough menacing guy with glasses), Ronnie Burns, our quarterback and Sammy Aston, a rather popular, outgoing kid. We won our class football championship and went on to play the champions of the 8th grade. They slaughtered us, but I still remember one play. I was in the defensive backfield when I went to pull the flag off of one of their players. The guy fell down, I pushed him, I don't know. But he was the same guy, Tony, who had bulled over me earlier in the football practice. And now he seemed so meek and mild.

I was so influenced by Danny Reid's muscles, that I bought a pair of 3 pound dumbbells and a muscle stretch device that is no longer made. I worked out with these devices in the hopes of somehow competing with the likes of Danny Reid. The stretch device had handles and I would put my foot through the handles and work my biceps.

My mother got a job with the Girl Scouts of America, which paid her little. Her friends were people who worked with her like Dorothy Canfield and Alma. Alma and her husband also owned movie theaters, and got us tickets to see such well-known first run films as *Pillow Talk, Operation*

Petty Coat, *Suddenly Last Summer,* and *North by North-west.* My sister Phoebe and I went to see these films.

My step-father, Al Ortega, got a job as a TV repairman. I remember seeing him once driving past the school in a TV repair pick-up truck. I think my mother became suspicious of Al Ortega when one day two agents showed up at out house at 29 Encanto while I was away, probably at the Encanto Park swimming pool. These agents told my mother that our family owed more than $3,000 for reasons I have never been able to find out.

AL, GONE

I do know that before Christmas, my mother confronted Al about this incident, and that he packed a suitcase and left us saying he would be back in two weeks, and that he had to go "find some money." I was not surprised when All never returned. Two weeks before Christmas, and I had a feeling Al was not coming back. I cannot say I missed him. As for my mother, she went to the Episcopal bishop, Bishop Kinsolving, for help. Bishop Kinsolving worked out a plan with the creditors. Paying food for us, paying rent, and paying off the creditors made life tough for my mother.

CHAPTER 10

EDMONDS, WASHINGTON – COULD HAVE BEEN CHICAGO

———

THE HEADLINES **in 1960**

- Democrat John F. Kennedy wins the U.S. Presidential Election after defeating Republican Richard Nixon. Kennedy became the first president and was the youngest person to have been elected into the highest office at the time.
- Togo, Cote D'Ivoire, Chad, Benin, Mauritania, Senegal, and the Central African Republic gain independence from France.
- The Organization of Petroleum Exporting Countries (OPEC) is created.
- The United States decides to send 3,500 U.S. troops to Vietnam.[1]

As it happened, in the spring of 1960, Mr. Timmerman of Jofa fabrics offered my mother a job in the headquarters' office in Chicago, paying her more than double of what she was making with the Phoenix Girl Scouts. Before that I continued my life in Phoenix until we left for good in June of 1960, at the conclusion of the school year. I must say, I rather enjoyed my time at Kenilworth School in Phoenix, although I ended up quitting the football team, the basketball team and the softball team.

I thought of myself as a pretty good athlete. But I guess I was still middle of the pack. Still, I was younger than any of my classmates in Phoenix. We had gotten used to the fact that Danny Reid was the fastest runner, the most powerful human being any of us had ever seen. Danny was in our class, the 7-1s. Bill Miller was not much of an athlete, but he was the fastest runner of the 7-2s. Mike Pensinger and Bob Watkins were the top athletes of the 7-3s.

I remember each morning, Coach Tamarin had us run around all four baseball diamonds. We'd finish where we started. I had started to run home each day, about 7 tenths of a mile, so I was used to running the distance. I had remembered how the horse Silky Sullivan had famously won races at Santa Anita by holding way back, trailing the field and then at the final turn, began to run all the other horses down. Well, I decided that this was how I would handle the run we had each morning in PE.

I kept my eye on who was leading and then right before the halfway point, I started to sprint. I gradually overtook guys until around the final turn me, Bill Miller and Danny Reid were in the lead. I overtook them but, with their sprinters speed, they responded to the challenge. I think we all three finished in a dead heat.

But one day in late spring, we were joined in the daily run by a kid who was being placed in the 7-3s on a trial basis, because he had gotten into trouble with the police. No one was told what he had done wrong, but we knew that he liked to smoke after school, even before school. His name was David Zilli, and he was a skinny kid, somewhat built for speed, I guess. Anyway, there he was one morning for our daily run. We took off and Zilli was way out in front. I employed my strategy, but when I got going, Zilli was already past the final turn. He won by a large margin, that skinny kid who smoked. I felt I was in the presence of an unusual talent, but in later years, I never heard about him at all.

I think I kept in touch with David Berner by letter writing. I learned that in my absence, he had become the starting shortstop to Koch fiberglass and even made the All-Star team. Meanwhile, I missed my final year of Little League, plus the half season of the earlier year.

SOFTBALL CAPTAIN

All in all, I never recovered from losing my dream of becoming a professional baseball player. In Phoenix, Arizona, we played softball, wearing gloves for fielding. I remember they made me captain again of this team, replacing Jim the tough guy. We won a playoff against the 7-

2s, and I remember Danny Reid had started the game as pitcher because he insisted he could do it, but he was not doing well. I called time and walked to the pitcher's area and took the ball from Danny. I then turned and brought in a soft but accurate-pitching kid, who was playing left field for us at that moment. His name was Mike Johnson. Mike was a little guy who came in and choked off their rally. We won the game.

Then, in the final playoff, against the 7-3s, I hit a home run to the opposite field off of Mike Pensinger. I came sliding into home for that one, and the catcher, Bob Watkins, Pensinger's close friend, was all over me, punching me. Coach Tamarin called me safe. Those were the two runs we scored and lost 5-2.

Around that time, I was playing for the school softball team. Before I quit that team, our group played a team from across town. Their pitcher was a black kid. I remember he struck me out on three fastball pitches. But soon after that, I quit the softball team. I remember asking if there was a Little League in all Phoenix, but they told me that there was none. And so, I had to face the fact that my 1960 Little League season was not going to happen.

BYE-BYE PHOENIX

When the school year was over, my mother, Phoebe and I went to the airport. Dorothy Canfield drove us, as by now we did not have a car of our own. My mother had asked us kids if we wanted to go with her to Chicago, or go back up to live with our grandparents. My sister and I both voted to live with our grandparents instead of moving to Chicago. Thus we decided we would not live in Chicago.

The temperature was upwards of 100 degrees in Phoenix that June day, and this was my first airplane flight. Later that week, the Phoenix temperature was 120 degrees. Knowing my tendency to throw up during long drives in a car, I remember my mother showing me where the air sick bag was in the airplane. I still remember holding it. My mother gave me dramamine, during the flight, I did not become air sick, thank goodness.

But I did have a reunion with my friend David Berner that summer. I think we had exchanged letters. I must have taken a bus from San Francisco to Corte Madera. In any event, we got together and I remember we went out into the street and I attempted to hit fungoes to David, and I showed off batting left-handed. I remember one ball I hit landed on a car, a baseball, not a softball. The car was not damaged.

Later that evening, I remember being at the Greyhound bus station, and Mrs. Berner hugging my mother good-bye. They had never known each other. That is why I remember it. We stayed two or three days at the Hensley's house. I think my sister and I went up to Seattle to stay at my Uncle Edgar and Aunt Winifred's house in Edmonds, Washington. And my mother took the bus to Chicago. I never saw my friend David Berner again.

· · ·

By this time, my grandparents had moved into small hut-like living quarters next to Aunt Winifred and Uncle Edgar's Edmonds house. I don't remember where my sister slept during that time, but I took a room on the second floor of Edgar and Winifred's house. I was enrolled in the Edmonds Junior High School, which was within walking distance from the house.

I remember watching television with my grandmother in the hut next to Aunt Winifred and Uncle Edgar's house. We watched Seattle Rainier baseball that summer, and I remember seeing a game against the San Diego Padres. For San Diego, I remember two players; Stan Jefferson and Floyd Robinson. Years later, I would see Floyd Robinson playing for the Chicago White Sox, a major league team. But at that time, 1960, he was still a young player with the minor league San Diego Padres.

One day, two boys came to the door of the hut asking for donations to their sandlot football team coming up in the fall. My grandfather answered the door and told them about me. I told him I was not interested. Baseball was my game, not football. My grandfather was somewhat embarrassed.

I recognized one of the kids. He was Brad Meyring. I think earlier that summer, soon after I arrived in Edmonds, I had heard about a Little League team in Edmonds. Coached by Brad's father, Mr. Meyring. I went to their practice and spoke with Mr. Meyring. I told him I was surprised they still had a league going. He at once put me up to bat against his son, Brad. Brad was throwing curve balls, and he struck me out.

YOU'RE ONE OF THEM MEXICAN KIDS?

After the inning, I went out to play left field. The kid next to me looked at me, with my dark tan from the Phoenix sunshine. He said, "You're one of them Mexican kids, aren't you?" A Mexican team had won the Little League World Series, and this guy thought I must be from one of the Mexican teams because my complexion was dark. I must have told him something like "No, I am an American kid, like you. I got dark from living in Phoenix."

Then, Mr. Meyring and one of his coaches began shouting at me to leave the field. I went home. I guess they wanted to see how well I could hit Brad's curve ball, and now they wanted me gone because I struck out. If I had hit Brad, they probably would have found a spot on the team for me. Partly because of this incident I was so negative when Brad and his friend Mike came to our door asking for donations for their upcoming football season.

WASHINGTON HUSKIES FOOTBALL

That fall, from the hut, I listened to the Washington Husky football broadcasts on radio given by announcer Rod Belcher. The year before, my grandmother had sent me news clippings about the Washington football team, defeating Utah State or University of Utah by a big score. Then on New Year's Day, still living in Phoenix, I watched the Washington Huskies play the University of Wisconsin

Badgers in the Rose Bowl. Even though Washington entered the game with a record of 9 wins against one loss, the Wisconsin Badgers were favored by one touchdown, or 7 points.

Wisconsin had something unheard-of back then: a black quarterback. His name was Sandy Stephens. And they had an outstanding player named Dale Hackbart. Hackbart would play in the defensive backfield with the Minnesota Vikings. But the Washington Huskies rolled over Wisconsin, surprising everyone by the score of 44-8. I had become a big fan and was anticipating a great season while I lived in Edmonds. Washington's best players had all been juniors during the earlier year. This meant that they would all be returning to play their senior season in 1960. I was excited and listened to every game.

I remember the Huskies dared to play the powerful Navy team in their third game of the season. Navy was considered one of the best teams in the nation in 1960. They had a little powerful running back named Joe Bellino. Bellino was one of the favorites to win the Heisman trophy as the best college player in the country. Washington also had a Heisman candidate in their quarterback and defensive back Bob Schloredt. Schloredt hailed from Gresham, Oregon.

In those days, college football players played both sides of the ball, that is, they played offense and defense.

· · ·

In the third game, Navy came into Husky Stadium in Seattle and were favored to beat Washington. I remember listening to the game. Washington scored and Fleming made the kick. Washington led 7-0. But Navy came right back and scored. Their kicker, Greg Mathers, missed the extra point; Washington 7, Navy 6. Then two more times, Washington got within the Navy 5 yard line. Instead of bringing in Fleming to kick an easy field goal, Washington went for the yardage on 4th down. They failed both times, and Navy took over. This happened twice in the first half. Navy was tough.

Then Washington scored a touchdown and led 14-6. Navy came right back and scored a touchdown, but missed the conversion; Washington 14, Navy 12. Meanwhile, the tough Navy team caused injuries to be sustained by some of Washington's best linemen. And so the game came down to the final 2 minutes. On 4th down, Schloredt went back to punt the ball. This would drive Navy back and probably ice the game for Washington. But Washinton's center had been injured, and a substitute center was hiking the ball back to Schloredt.

I remember Rod Belcher announcing that the ball hiked back to Schloredt went over his head and back towards the Washington goal line. Schloredt went back and fell on the ball, but the ball belonged to Navy, 1st and 10. I think the ball was on the Washington 20, and Navy had Bellino to run the ball. But, miraculously, the Washington defense held Navy to no gains on their first three plays and now, 4th down. Navy had no choice but to try a 38 yard field goal, or lose the game to Washington. Greg Mather, who had failed earlier on his extra point try from point blank range, came onto the field. Mather kicked the ball, and somehow it cleared inside the goal post. Navy now led, 15-14, and when Washington got the ball back, they could not score with virtually seconds left on the clock. Time ran out and Washington lost a game they should have won.

Then came the UCLA game, I think this was the 5th game of the season, and in Husky Stadium. In this game, Bob Schloredt, playing defensive back, went up to block a pass and came down on his collarbone. He broke his collarbone and was out for the rest of the season. I remember reading that the trainer said that if Washington made it to the Rose Bowl, Schloredt would be able to play.

Although UCLA had future pros Billy Kilmer and Jimmie Johnson playing for them, the Huskies held on to win, 10-8. In the meantime, the Huskies visited Stanford and won, and visited USC in the Coliseum and clobbered them 34-0.

TERRIBLE TERRY BAKER

On one of the following weeks, I listened at Uncle Edgar's house on their radio to the game from Multnomah Stadium in Corvallis, Oregon to the Washington vs. Oregon State game. Oregon State ran a single wing attack, and their quarterback was a young sophomore named Terry Baker, who soon became known as "Terrible Terry Baker" and who, one day, as a senior, would win the Heisman Trophy.

. . .

Two facts I noted in this game. One was that Washington's quarterback was now Bob Hivner, who was probably a better pure passer than Schloredt, but not the athlete that Schloredt was. Hivner had been ahead of Schloredt when they were sophomores, but Hivner had gotten injured. Schloredt replaced Hivner and the rest was history; until now. Hivner was now leading Washington up against the powerful Oregon State Beavers. And the second thing became clear. Washington could not stop Terrible Terry Baker. At halftime, the score was something like Oregon State 22, Washington 7.

I remember crying at halftime and when my grandfather, who was there, asked me how the game was going, I tearfully replied that the game was not going well. Washington was way behind and losing the game. My grandfather said, "They'll come back." And he walked away. I did not believe him.

I do not remember the details. I know that Washington did come back. But "Terrible Terry" led Oregon State to still another score, which was something like Oregon State 29, Washington 16. But in the end, the Huskies miraculously responded and the final score was Washington 30, Oregon State 29. Like the battles in earlier wars, Gettysburg, Verdun, etc., the world will little note nor long remember what happened on that football field.

Also, at this time a 2nd cousin of mine, Roger, pulled the head off of my longtime doll friend, Sammy. Yes, Sammy's head came off in a tug of war between me and Roger. I was heart broken. Aunt Winnifred came to the rescue and managed to sew Sammy's head back on. But alas, I had outgrown Sammy, and he no longer played a roll in my life.

In the next week or so, we had moved into a new house, a half block away from the Edmonds Junior High School, where I attended the 8th grade. I remember that my grandmother had taken ill, and my Uncle Bim was visiting us. The three of us were listening to the game at Husky Stadium against the University of Oregon. Somehow, the Oregon Ducks, with their All American Dave Grayson in the backfield, was defeating Washington by the score of 6-0.

Hivner could not move the team the way that Schloredt had. We had great black athletes like George Fleming, Ray Jackson, Joe Jones and Charlie Mitchell. Two of these guys would go on to be professional football players, Fleming a revered state senator, and Jackson a revered police officer. But Oregon led 6-0 right down to the final minute or so.

Washington had the ball in their own territory. Hivner went back to pass and discovered Don McKeta, the 26 year-old ex Marine crossing the Oregon secondary. Hivner had always been an outstanding passer. Now he led McKeta. Grayson, the future All Pro defensive back thought McKeta would run out of bounds, and pulled up, so he could prevent any chance of a penalty. And McKeta, cleverly stopped at the sideline and pivoted up field. He ran like hell, with Grayson in pursuit, and scored the tying touchdown. Fleming, who would go on to kick for the professional Oakland Raiders the next season, reliably kicked the extra point.

The final score was Washington 7, Oregon 6. The next and final game was in the mud at Washington State. In this game, again the Huskies trailed 7-0 for most of the game. Washington scored, but they needed two points to go ahead. Enter Kermit Jorgensen, who somehow threw the winning pass into the end zone. And here the final score was Washington 8, Washington State 7. And so, it would be on to next year's January 1, 1961, Rose Bowl, which the Huskies won.

CLARINET, THE BEGINNINGS

This was the school year, at Edmonds Junior High School, that I began to play the clarinet. I don't remember why I chose to be in the beginners' music class with Mr. Reid as the school band leader, our teacher. I think I had seen Benny Goodman on TV. At the local music store in Edmonds, we rented a Selmer Bundy clarinet, made of ebonite. There were eight of us in the beginner class, I remember. And I learned the rudiments of playing the clarinet. I would practice at home.

As it happened, after the Oregon game that the Huskies won, my grandmother was ill and was in a coma at the hospital. It turned out, although no one seemed to think it remarkable at the time, I was the last person to speak with her.

. . .

In those horrible days, I still was a chronic bed wetter. I had to have a rubberized sheet placed under my normal bed sheeting. I slept in the same bedroom with my grandfather. And because by this time, being an 8th grader, though still 12 years old, I showered each morning in the shower newly installed in the basement, to counteract the smell of dried urine on my body. I was terribly afraid the other kids would notice.

I remember also our 8th grade class led by Mrs. Reid, no relation to the band teacher of the same name. Mrs. Reid did have halitosis. The girl in the class that I had a crush on at the time was Suzy Miller. I thought she was attractive, though I would never dare speak to her, except formally.

I went out for the 8th grade school basketball team. I got the impression that the so-called coach of the team did not know much about basketball. In any event, he cut me from the team the first day. There were guys who were on the team I could beat one-on-one. If I had stayed at the school for the 9th grade, I think I would have proven myself. The coach of the 9th grade team, Coach Arndt, I felt, knew basketball pretty well.

That fall, we listened to the World Series. It seemed impossible at the time that the Pittsburgh Pirates could stand up to the powerful New York Yankees. The Yankees in the games they won, slaughtered the Pirates. The

Pirates' pitcher Vinegar Bend Mizell was overrun by the Yankees hitters. Bob Friend, Vern Law, Harvey Haddix and reliever Elroy Face pitched for the Pirates. They had Roberto Clemente, Hal Smith and Bill Mazeroski, but even with these stars, the Yankees with Mickey Mantle, Roger Maris, Yogi Berra, and Elston Howard, seemed superior.

With real astonishment we listened as Bill Mazeroski broke open a seemingly sure Yankee win with his gigantic long home run to seal the win for Pittsburgh. I doubted there would ever again be a game like that, and in October 1960, the Pittsburgh Pirates won the World Series, and I cheered them on. Anything to beat those hated Yankees.

In school, I was doing well that fall in gym class, as taught by Mr. Waggoner. Mr. Waggoner seemed to think that I was some kind of special athletic talent, in football and basketball. I had been well-trained for this my earlier year in Phoenix, Arizona under Mr. Tamerin.

A FINAL GOOD-BYE

Anyway, back to the night in late November 1960 when I spoke with my grandmother. For some reason, preventing me from wetting the bed, I awoke at around 2:15 am to go pee. I was happy about this. This could be the end of my bed-wetting problem! It had been plaguing me for so long. As I left the bathroom and about to turn the corner to head back to my bed, I thought I heard my grandmother calling from the living room. In those days, my grandmother voluntarily slept on the living room couch so that my sister could have her own bedroom.

I went to the living room and spoke, "Grandma? What is it?"

She replied that she thought she had left a lighted cigarette somewhere on her bedding, and she was worried that it might cause a fire. I looked for and found the cigarette, and sure enough, still burning. But I put the cigarette out in her ashtray and saw that no damage resulted, no fire started. And, so I told her, "Grandma, I found the cigarette, and I put it out. Don't worry."

And she said, "Okay. Thank you, honey."

Those were the last words my grandmother ever spoke to anyone. The next morning as I left for school, I noticed that she was apparently still sleeping on the couch, and so I went through the main door and on to school. When I returned from school, they told me that my grandmother had been removed to a hospital and that she was in a coma. I was never allowed to visit her. She died, I think two or three days later.

My grandmother was born September 5, 1893, in Fergus Falls, Minnesota. She died November 24, 1960, in Edmonds, Washington. This was around the time John F.

Kennedy, whom my family supported, was elected President of the United States. I remember Mrs. Reid, our teacher, was firmly a Nixon supporter.

We had watched the debates on TV. We thought Kennedy had a funny accent and I thought Nixon was pretty good. After all, Nixon was a Californian and spoke more or less like us. But we still wanted Kennedy.

Near the end of 1960, we had a Christmas celebration of sorts in our 8th grade class. Mrs. Reid organized a class drawing, the object of which was that each of us drew somebody's name, and we were supposed to buy that person a Christmas gift. Mrs. Reid gave us the choice of giving the gift anonymously or showing our names. Wouldn't you know it, but I drew Susie Miller's name.

IF YOU KNEW SUSIE

I was not about to reveal to Susie Miller that I was the one about to give her a gift, so, there was my sister Phoebe to the rescue. Phoebe went to the store and got me a little bottle of perfume and wrapped it up nice and wrote To: Susie Miller on the gift tag, without attaching my name.

I always felt afterwards that Susie Miller guessed that I got her the gift, but I guess I will never know.

CHAPTER 11

SAN FRANCISCO – MY HEART DIDN'T SEEM TO MATTER

THE HEADLINES **in 1961**

- Outgoing President Eisenhower issues warning of a "military industrial complex" developing in America
- President Kennedy establishes Peace Corps
- Cuban exiles fail in their bid to invade Cuba through the Bay of Pigs; President Kennedy accepts responsibility
- Soviets build wall dividing East and West Berlin
- Nazi leader Adolf Eichmann tried in Israel, found guilty
- "Freedom Riders" travel throughout the South to test and promote integration measures; are assaulted and beaten[1]

The year 1961 came, and I was still in Edmonds, finishing up my 8th grade year. One thing that had happened which had an important impact on my life was the following. I used to love to eat Wheaties, the breakfast cereal. One of the items on the box I read mentioned a contest that I could enter. Somehow, I convinced my grandparents or perhaps my Aunt Winifred that I should enter this contest.

From the Post Office I bought 18 post cards and sent them all into the contest. I was much surprised weeks later when I was notified that I had won something. In fact, I had won a new basketball. The prize came to me, and I took it to school to have Mr. Waggoner fill the ball with the proper amount of air. And then I began to practice after school.

BASKETBALL WAS IMPORTANT

A schoolyard up a hill not far from where I lived, had a nice outdoor basketball court with steel chains for nets. I saw on TV Bill Sharman of the Boston Celtics talking about the one-hand set shot. Sharman was very accurate and until I saw that interview, I had copied Dolph Shayes's two-hand set shot. But after seeing Sharman, I began shooting the one-handed shot.

And I practiced every day 100 free throws. My best score was 67 free throws made out of 100. I practiced other exercises of my own invention, one of which was to focus on doing everything I could do with my right hand, to be able to do it with my left hand. I still had my three pound weights from Phoenix, Arizona, that I carried in my hands and ran up and down the court with, leaping at the basket.

My mother hated the job she had working for a doctor's office in Seattle. When my grandmother died, my mother had to resign the job she loved at Jofa in Chicago and come to live with us in Edmonds. All because of us kids that she felt she had to do this. If we had expressed a desire to move with her to Chicago, how different my life would have become!

But move to Edmonds my mother did, burning her bridges to the world of Jofa in Chicago as she did so. It also meant that she began to set her sights on San Francisco and moving there, as she still hated Seattle, the city of her birth, with a passion. And so, we knew that the next year would be spent in San Francisco, as soon as the school year in Edmonds ended in June 1961.

Around this time my sister Phoebe had a visit from Silvia Crecelius. We had already absorbed the news that Silvia's younger brother and my friend, Brian, had been killed on Mount Rainier. Brian and the family were on a hiking trip on the mountain, and Brian told the family he wanted to take a different trail heading in the same direction. And on this trail, he had fallen to his death. I had not seen nor heard from Brian in years, but his passing was something I will never forget. He was such a good boy.

· · ·

In the meantime, spring 1961 came around and so did baseball season. I had stopped my basketball practices by that April, as the NBA playoffs finished. And so, as a now 13 year-old, I paid attention to the fact that spring meant baseball tryouts for the Babe Ruth League. Instead of maintaining my Gino Cimoli batting style, that I employed as an 11 year-old, I now got it into my head to learn to switch hit, batting from the left side as well as the right side. I figured if Mickey Mantle good learn switch hitting, so could I.

This meant, I had to face good pitching batting left-handed. While true, that I had worked on batting left-handed a bit in the past year or so, I had been out of organized baseball for a year and a half, and my body had grown. When it came to the tryouts, it seemed there were no left-handed pitchers for me to bat against. This meant that every time I came up to bat, I would have to bat left-handed, and I was not good enough batting left-handed. And so, I did not receive the opportunity to play.

The odd thing was, as an outfielder, I proved myself to be the best they had. I could catch anything. I had decided to use Willie Mays's basket catch philosophy. That went pretty well for me most of the time. And another thing I remember. We used to want to race home on the nights that the TV program "My Three Sons" was on. During the first two seasons, this program was on, it was directed by a man named Peter Tewksbury. And the program was wonderfully imaginative. After Tewksbury left the program in the fall of 1963, the program was no longer worth watching, at least for me.

. . .

The Babe Ruth League was the next step up from Little League. Meant for boys age 13 to 15. We represented Edmonds, and played teams from Lynwood, Mountlake Terrace, and other regional teams. Our Edmonds team was divided into two teams—sort of major league, for the older boys, and minor league for the younger boys. We had good curveball pitchers like Russ Meyer, our oldest and best player, Brad Meyring and Terry Gibbons. I could probably have beaten any of those kids in basketball, but I had given up basketball in favor of baseball, because at that time of year, no one was playing basketball. Everyone was focused on baseball.

And so, in the games, I was often relegated to playing bat boy. I made the mistake one day of sitting on the bench between our main coach, Daryl, and a friend of mine, John Dinkel. The mistake was that I told John my sad story of trying to be a switch hitter, and thus denying myself the ability to prove myself to the coaches, Daryl and Mike. We had one kid on the team who played shortstop, his last name being Howe. Howe's sister was a friend of my sister, and they both came to one of our games. It so happened that the opposing pitcher was a left-hander, so I could bat right-handed. My sister and Miss Howe both cheered me on as I came up to the plate. I slammed a pitch on a line down the left field line, but I had hit a foul ball. After that, I do not remember what happened but I either made an out or received a walk. The season ended that summer, and we moved down to San Francisco.

SAN FRANCISCO, HERE I COME

I packed my clarinet, which in the meantime, I had bought from the music store in Edmonds. My grandfather used my savings account money to help pay for the instrument, I might add. That summer, I did not practice the clarinet at all.

We drove down to San Francisco in a second-hand 1951 Chevrolet. I do not remember this trip at all. Once in San Francisco, we found a place to live on Seventh Avenue, within walking distance of the junior high school, Roosevelt Junior High School, on the corner of Arguello and Geary, about eight city blocks away. This school, today known as Roosevelt Middle School, was where such luminaries as Johnny Mathis had attended in the early 1950s.

Once installed at Roosevelt Junior High, I learned that they had baseball season there in the fall. As I had by this time baseball spikes, shoes for baseball playing, I decided to go out for the team. I came in with the idea of continuing to switch hit, thus necessitating that I bat left-handed most of the time. The majority of the pitchers were, of course, right-handers. I also found that as I had grown bigger, my base-ball shoes did not fit me anymore.

Coach Nelson asked us to write down on a piece of paper what our aspirations as players on the Roosevelt Junior High team might be. I remember writing down my frustrations at trying to be a switch hitter, and never getting a chance to play in Edmonds, on the Babe Ruth second team.

One day, Coach Nelson announced that we would be playing another junior high school team across town. We all had to take a city bus across town to be at this game. Well, at that time, I had never ridden a city bus in my life; at least, not by myself. And so, being almost terrified at the thought of taking a bus, I did not go to the game. The next day, at practice, the coach chewed me out. "I looked to play you, and you weren't there!" he chastised me. I was afraid to tell anyone that I never had taken a city bus anywhere, and I was afraid to mention this out loud.

There was this kid named John Nious. For some reason, John walked over to where I was sitting and ordered me to stand up. I stood up. Nious, who had this metallic ring on one of the fingers of his right hand, proceeded to slug me right on the left collar bone. I had no idea why he did this. He just pounded me. And I accepted this for some reason, and did not retaliate whatsoever, neither with fists, nor words. I sat down and stared straight ahead. John Nious walked away. I had a welt on my collarbone that took days to heal.

Meanwhile, I tried to join the school band at Roosevelt and I barely played my clarinet, having started the year before at Edmonds Junior High, as an 8th grader. Well, school systems are different depending on where you are. Edmonds, Washington was a small town, while San Francisco, two states and some 800 miles away, was a major city. The Roosevelt Junior High band instructor, Mr. Marvin Nelson, was an accomplished trumpet player, he actually was a member of the Oakland Symphony trumpet section. And he was a strict band master. He was much more ambitious about the music program than had been Mr. Reid up in Edmonds Junior high.

I remember when enrolling in Roosevelt Junior High, there was a tough Assistant Principal. The Assistant Principals in both junior high schools tended to be the disciplinarians. The fact that they were disciplinarians prompts me to remember an incident which had taken place in Edmonds Junior high in 1961 as an 8th grader.

Our Math teacher in Edmonds was a Mr. Fitzpatrick. One day, I think I may have been day dreaming, Mr. Fitzpatrick decided to send me to the Assistant Principal's office. He said to me something like "Phil, you don't look like you are studying. Why don't you go down to Mr. Clemens's office," So I gathered my books and went down to see Mr. Clemens, the assistant Principal. I remember that Mr. Clemens had a cracked glass plate covering his desk. My first thought was, I wondered how that crack had occurred.

I remember Mr. Clemens saying to me, "So you wouldn't study for Mr. Fitzpatrick, huh?" I replied that I had not been doing anything wrong. I did not realize it at the time, but the assistant principal's job was probably to support his teachers, no matter if that teacher was right or wrong. In this case, I felt Mr. Fitzpatrick was wrong, but being a kid, I did not feel I could fight with Mr. Clemens. He glared at me and shouted, "Do you get enough to eat at home?" I felt insulted and I wanted to rebel against this guy. But instead, I played along and said I was sorry, etc. He let me go without further punishment.

I also remember that year, in that math class, I had a friend named Dave Johnson. I remember bringing Dave up to my basketball court and beating him in a one-on-one game with a series of left-handed hooks and set shots. I remember the Friday before Easter, Dave saying to everyone in the Math class as Mr. Fitzpatrick let us go, "Don't let the Easter bunny eat ya!"

But then, around that time, Dave stopped being my friend. It seemed he purposely ignored me. I didn't know what was wrong. Was it my breath? I had halitosis and was unaware of it? I did not know why he stopped being friendly towards me.

MATH? UCISM? ME?

In the last week of math class, before summer break, Mr. Fitzpatrick was somewhat excited to administer us a test to see how we might qualify for UCISM math in the 9th grade next year. Evidently, UCISM was a new program of mathematics teaching from the University of Illinois in 1961. I remember taking the test, and later I somehow got a look at the results listing. Mr. Fitzpatrick had listed my name near the bottom and placed triple question marks next to my name. He told me I had done well on the test, and because my performance in his class was otherwise mediocre, he was questioning my qualifications for UCISM.

Well, this was a moot point for the 9th grade, as I now sat with my mother and grandfather in the assistant principal's office at Roosevelt Junior High School, San Francisco, in September 1961. When I mentioned the math situation to the assistant principal, he got somewhat excited, because although Roosevelt Junior High was not affiliated in any way with UCISM, they did have a special program with a new system of mathematics offered by Yale University. And so, the assistant principal, made sure I was enrolled in that Yale math class. This placed me with all the top scoring students in the school.

Roosevelt Junior High School tried to segment its students based upon their intelligence, which were based upon test scores, I guess. As I had come from another school district, in another state, the assistant principal was at a loss on my placement. He put me in the top math class, but placed me in the 1C to 1D level, the mediocre kids, in English and Social Studies.

Our Home Room teacher at Roosevelt Junior High, whom I met for the first time in September 1961, was a Mr. Pluette. In our Home Room were such fellow students as Kim Greathouse, Penny Foster, Gale Gara, Steve Black, Francisco Olaje, Howard Yano, and some black students—Connie Glover, an angry black big kid named John, and a gentle but gifted athlete named Jewell. Connie Glover's younger brother, Danny Glover, later became a prominent actor who starred in Hollywood films.

The so-called smart kids were in the 1A and 1B classes. We less smart kids were placed in the 1C to 1D level. They also had 2A through 2D, and this is where they placed most of the black kids, kids like Jewell. A few of the smarter black kids were placed in our 1C and 1D level, kids like Jean Sample, Connie Glover, and the angry guy named John.

But the assistant principal could not guarantee my playing in the band. According to the rules, anyone in the 9th grade could not play in the Intermediate Band. I would have to qualify for the Advanced Band or not play in any band. And this would be up to an audition for the band teacher, Marvin Nelson.

LAST CHAIR – 18TH OUT OF 18

I went up to play for Mr. Nelson. He felt that I was not good enough for the Advanced Band, but I was a 9th grader, not eligible for the Intermediate Band. As he had five 3rd clarinet players, and he needed a 6th person to fill the last chair, he placed me at the last chair of the 3rd clarinetists. His organized Advanced Band now had 18 clarinetists, and I was now number 18, the last chair of the whole section.

This junior high school was better organized than Edmonds Junior High had been. For the first time in my life, I had

Jewish, Black, Chinese, Russian and Japanese-heritage classmates. Oh, in Phoenix at the Kenilworth School, we did have some Jewish kids, like Eddie Yoblonski. But here in San Francisco, there was a real community of Jews in attendance at Roosevelt Junior High. There was Steve Snow, Ricky Greenspan, Gale Gara, Eddie Hassid, Todd Schneider, Joe Mevorah, Rachel Milstein and others. They were all great people, and, my friends.

I remember this red-haired kid in gym class named Greg Klink, who was a real bully, and he was not Jewish. Once in gym class, Klink smiled this grin at some guy smaller than him, and put his fist up to the kid's face. One day we saw Klink stretched out on a rubbing table behind a closed off section of the gym dressing room. Evidently, he had run afoul with some high school kid who knocked some sense into him.

Sometimes at Roosevelt Junior High, we played intramural basketball games at lunchtime. As my mother had reunited with the Hensleys, Guy Hensley had taken me out and bought me a beautiful pair of Florsheim loafers. The problem with this was the fact that I had to play in the games with those loafers. Howard Yano, our Home Room team organizer had begged me to play. The gym, so I thought, was off limits during lunchtime, so I could not change into sneakers. And playing ball, I soon wore holes in the soles of these loafers. I was mortified. What would I tell Guy Hensley? Oh, God! He bought me those shoes!

. . .

I remember making a little jump shot from the side of the basket. Gale Gara, who was from our home room, cheering us on, called me out as that shot swished in. She was surprised I was so good! On another play, I was hagging a bit into the forecourt, no defenders in front of me. And big John, the angry black kid saw me and whipped a pass as hard as he could throw it directly at me. I pretended this was normal, caught the ball and went in for a lay up. I think John probably thought that the hard pass would overwhelm me, and I would drop the ball. Well, that did not happen; sorry, John.

I also remember a time when Bill Businius, the school's head basketball coach, was also our gym teacher. One day he had us, one at a time, go against his stop watch and run dribbling the ball, and shooting layups at three different baskets. After I took my turn, he looked at his watch and like, he didn't believe it. Like I had set some kind of record. He felt something was wrong, and he asked me to go again. I went again, going even faster, but I blew the final layup, missed the shot entirely, and that was that. Mr. Businius never bothered me again. Later I would see Businius refereeing college games on TV. He knew his basketball.

When I first got to San Francisco, my mother resumed her relationships with people she knew well. She got a job managing an office for orthopedic surgeons. She had had so much experience doing this that she had little trouble getting a pretty good job. Living right down the street from us on 7th Avenue was Yvonne Bashta and her daughter, Vicky.

ROMANCE WAS IN THE AIR, BUT NOT FOR ME

My mother knew Yvonne as a professional working as a medical assistant with the orthopedic surgeons my mother worked for in the 1950s. It so happened that Vicky Bashta was one year ahead of me at school and played bassoon. She was a pretty good player, and had gone to Roosevelt Junior High, and had played for Mr. Nelson, the band director. Now she was at Lowell High School and I think she was a little sweet on me. That is, I think she wanted a romantic attachment with me. But I wanted none of it. I did not find her attractive, at all.

Vicky told me that Mr. Pluette, our home room teacher, had once been a bassoonist with the San Francisco Symphony. Wow! What a gig, right? I could not figure out how or why he was now a teacher at a Junior High School and no longer, according to Vicky, a bassoonist. I never asked him about it, like why he was a teacher and what he actually taught. He and I had little to do with each other.

I should mention that in my home room, at first I was somewhat befriended by another new kid named Steve Black. But after a week or so, Steve determined that I was not "in crowd" material, and he dropped me as a friend. In that home room class, though, there was some romance in the air. I was sweet on Penny Foster, who sat at the head of the row next to mine. She was the girl that I liked, but like with Suzy Miller before her, and Penny Craig in Phoenix, I never revealed to any of them how I felt about them. And then there was Gale Gara. Gale was a Jewish girl with braces on her teeth, and she decided I was the guy she wanted a relationship with. I was attracted to Penny Foster, not to Gale Gara. I think I seldom spoke to Penny. But Gale, I talked with. I had to because she was always smiling and talking to me.

At one point, Gale invited me to a dance at the local Jewish Community Center. I said I would go. On a Friday night I remember piling into our 1951 Chevrolet and my mother driving me to the Jewish Community Center. I got out of the car, and walked into the building. But I did not see any person nor did I hear any sounds of music coming from anywhere. I turned around and left the building. My mother was still outside in the car. I got in and we drove home.

I don't remember that I ever explained all this to Gale. She concluded that I was anti-Jewish. It wasn't true, one of my best friends in the school was Eddie Hassid. We did a lot of stuff together and I even visited his house and had lunch with his parents. That whole family was bilingual French and English. My best friends in the school were Denis Englander and Bill Chester. Denis was also bilingual French and English. His dad was the head of the English department at Lowell High School. His mom was French. And then there was Bill Chester. I liked Bill a lot too. He and Denis were both members of the Advanced band. I forget what Bill played. I think Alto Clarinet, but I am no longer sure of that. Denis played clarinet.

· · ·

I also signed up for Latin class. I enjoyed that a bit and did well in the class. The final class of the day. My mother had recommended that I study Latin because so much of English, as well as other languages, depended on Latin.

But the most important thing that happened to me at Roosevelt Junior High was my acclimation to the rigors of the Advanced Band. Mr. Nelson was, for me anyway, an inspiring teacher. It turned out, he played trumpet professionally in the Oakland Symphony Orchestra. He would test us every week on the parts we had in our music folders. And with each test, I began to move up. Pretty soon, I was the lead chair of the Third Clarinets. And Mr. Nelson held after school challenges twice a week. I signed up for each one and pretty soon, by Christmas Holidays in December, I was with the Second Clarinet section.

CHAPTER 12

THE CLARINET BECOMES MY NICHE

THE HEADLINES **in 1962**

- John Glenn becomes the first American to orbit the Earth in February of 1962
- Cuban Missile Crisis when USSR plans to deploy Missiles in Cuba brings the world to the brink of world war,
- Marilyn Monroe serenades President Kennedy on his birthday.
- Rioting on University of Mississippi campus following Black student James Meredith attempting to enroll
- The Space Needle an observation tower in Seattle, Washington is completed
- Marilyn Monroe is found dead on August 5 after apparently overdosing on sleeping pills[1]

When January came, I was soon leading the second clarinet section. Now there were four people, the first clarinetists ahead of me, to challenge. I challenged the 4th chair guy and won. The same happened with the 3rd and 2nd chair guys. Now I was next to the King, Ken Wiggins, a tall guy who was judged to be the best player of any section in the band. Evidently, Ken's mother was Arabic. I never asked him about his family, but Ken was proper and dignified. I think I tried to grab something one time out of his hand, and he looked at me and retorted "Try that again and see what happens." Whatever I had done, I apologized and certainly never did it again.

One day after school, ever the organizer, I got the guys to come and play full court basketball on the playground of Angelo Rossi playground, which was a half block from our school. I remember Ken Wiggins and Bill Chester were among the players. It turned out, Ken, like with everything else he tried, was a damned good basketball player. But I seemingly wanted to show off. On one play, I drove the length of the court with Ken Wiggins in hot pursuit. I went up for a left-hand hook shot layup and the ball cleared over Ken Wiggins's try to block it. I scored, and felt triumphant.

Ken also played tenor sax in the dance band. He took clarinet lessons from a Mr. Cicerone downtown in the basement of Sherman Clay in San Francisco. Soon, I began taking lessons with Mr. Cicerone, too. It cost me $3.50 per lesson. Also, Ken and I, being the first two clarinets, were now invited to play in the orchestra, which was otherwise solely string instruments, directed by Mr. Johansen. And I think Ken played a Noblet clarinet, a French made wooden clarinet. Not the best in the world, but a lot better than my cheap plastic Selmer Bundy. Kenneth sounded better than I did, and he could beat me on tone quality.

THE MAGNIFICENT CHALLENGE

Came the after school challenge where I went up against Ken Wiggins. And I beat him. I remember Mr. Nelson saying, "He beat you, Ken." The next morning at 8 AM I sat in the first chair. I remember oboist Glenn Kajiama and bassoonist Dennis Chin did not believe that I belonged there and tried to get me to move to the second chair. I stayed where I was and Ken came in and took the second chair. Kajiama and Chin could not believe it. They were astounded.

Ken and I went on to challenge each other a total of twelve times. I won six challenges, he won six challenges. On the final challenge day, i could have challenged him and perhaps won, but I was sick with a bad cold and absent from school those final three days. And so Ken finished first and at the school assembly, he was awarded with the best musician pin. Vicky Bashta later told me that Mr. Nelson fretted and could not decide whether to give me the pin over Ken because I had come so far. But alas, Mr. Nelson made his decision, and Ken got the award.

After all, I was now a teenager. My 14th birthday came and went, January 18. I do not remember the celebration, but I am sure my mother made it nice for me. I still slept in the bedroom with my grandfather. I also practiced the clarinet in this room. I got music from the San Francisco Public Library. I remember taking out the Brahms Sonata opus 120, #2. I was playing the part and I remember that some parts did not make sense to me.

I bought sheet music that I still own from a music store, near Sherman Clay. The music book has a green cover, and inside the book I learned the Spohr clarinet concerto #1, the Mozart Concerto, the Weber Concertos and the Weber Concertino. I was playing everything on a Bb clarinet. I had little idea of what an A clarinet would look like. I did not know that Mozart composed his clarinet Concerto for an A clarinet, so I practiced it on the Bb clarinet.

My Mother Mary Pallett, Photographer Martin
Allison, Corinne (standing) and Grandpa, 1962
— Photo by the Author.

I think the sweetest moment of my time at Roosevelt Junior High came when, on the last day of school, we played a softball game on a location near the back end of the school, a field that I had not known existed. Glenn Kajiama, the band oboist, was the organizer of the game. I came up to him and asked him where I should play, and he looked at me and said, "Anywhere you want." I felt incredibly respected at that moment, and I never forgot it. But there were more challenges coming.

What I did that summer, I don't remember. I remember starting Summer School, which took place at another Junior High School in San Francisco. I was worried that our Latin class had not finished the Latin Year One book. But I stopped going to Summer School a week after it started. I know we moved from the place on Seventh Avenue to a nice first floor apartment in Stonestown, San Francisco, and this location was within walking distance of the new Lowell High School. I would be enrolling there in the fall.

Before I left Roosevelt, though, I remember Mr. Herbert Welch coming to Roosevelt Junior High. Mr. Welch was the music director at George Washington High School, the school for which Roosevelt Junior High was one of the main feeder schools. Almost every student who graduated from Roosevelt Junior High went to Washington. For example, both Denis Englander and Bill Chester went on to Washington. As did Glen Kajiama, Dennis Chin and Gale Gara. But there were 10 of us from Roosevelt Junior High who chose to go to Lowell. Among the 10 were Kim Greathouse, Eddie Hassid and Jean Sample.

Phil's graduation picture, Roosevelt Junior High School, June 1962 Photo by Mary Pallett

Also, during this time, I had auditioned for Georg Salner, a fellow who was an oboist in the Oakland Symphony Orchestra. Mr. Salner also had a position teaching music in the San Francisco School system, and he was in charge of the wind section for the San Francisco All City high school orchestra. Soon, I would be joining bassoonist Vicky Bashta not only in the Lowell High School Orchestra, but also the All-City Orchestra.

I played for Mr. Salner, and he accepted me into the orchestra for the 1962-63 season. I also remember playing in the new apartment in Stonestown in one of the two empty bedrooms. I practiced the Spohr first clarinet concerto and was thrilled by the echoey sound. Furniture had yet to be delivered to the new apartment.

During this time, I was in the market for a new clarinet. I wanted to get a new Selmer or Buffet clarinet. I heard these were the best instruments at the time. First, I tried a Selmer clarinet in Albert Cicerone's studio located in the basement of the Sherman Clay music store. A Sherman Clay salesman brought in the clarinet in a case and left it with me and Mr. Cicerone. I put the clarinet together and for some reason or other, I did not like the clarinet. I packed it away, the salesman later came in, and Mr. Cicerone told the salesman that I did not like the clarinet. The salesman took the clarinet case away. I remember the salesman was abrupt and did not say anything to me.

Not long after my mother accompanied me to a music store in Oakland called "The House of Woodwinds." This store was owned and operated by a Mr. George Koregelos, who was also a highly recognized wind instrument repair man. Mr. Koregelos had five instruments for me to try. I think there were two Buffets and three LeBlanc clarinets. LeBlanc was the third favorite of the top three clarinets in the world at that time.

I loved the key action on the LeBlanc clarinets, and Mr. Koregelos agreed, but sound wise I preferred one of the Buffets. Mr. Koregelos again agreed. He played both instruments for me, and he sounded terrific. He said he had told the LeBlanc representative that the key action on the LeBlancs was indeed superior, but the LeBlanc clarinets could not match the Buffet for clarity of tone. I sounded better on this Buffet than I had on my Bundy plastic clarinet. My mother wrote a check for $320 and we bought the new Buffet.

· · ·

There was one bit of bad news about living at 415 Winston Drive in Stonestown. Above the ground-floor apartment we now inhabited lived a San Francisco fireman whose duty took place at night. He slept in the afternoons when I needed to practice. And these people complained to the apartments administrative office with a formal complaint. As a result, I was not allowed to practice in our apartment. To the rescue came my grandfather, who, being a retired Episcopal priest, had established a relationship with the local St. Francis Episcopal church, not terribly far from where we lived in Stonestown.

The result of this was that I was allowed to have a key to the church's classroom area, and I was allowed to practice in one of the basement classrooms whenever I wanted. My grandfather also supplied a large leather carrying case in which I could keep all my music. I left this case in the class-room, as I would be using the room every day.

That fall, I also enrolled in Lowell High School. I was now a 14 year-old sophomore. I believe now I made a mistake in not being more aggressive in tackling academic responsibili-ties. All I was interested in seemed to be to become the best clarinetist in the world. The only class I remember doing well in was Geometry, for which I attained a B. But Lowell High School had so many famous graduates. Leaders in entertainment like Carol Channing, and other public figures.

ACCUSED OF PLAGIARISM

In English that fall, I was indifferent to be assigned to the class of Mr. Lindner. Mr. Lindner came across as a sort of intellectual. He was tall, with a rather small head, and he wore glasses. Our assignment for most of the class was to read Shakespeare's Julius Caesar. Also, we were to turn in a one-paragraph book report on a novel of our choice. He called this report a critique of the novel. Welcome to high school English! I chose to read and write my critique on Oliver Twist, by Charles Dickens.

I was younger than everyone else in the class, and Mr. Lindner seemed to think that I was one of the clowns, or iconoclastic low-lifes in the class. I remember a beautiful girl with teased-up hair who sat behind me, Charlene B. When I told my fellow clarinetist classmate Dennis M. that Charlene was the prettiest girl in my class, his reply was, "Oh, Charlene's been fuc*ing for years."

Also in the class were a couple of buddies who hung together, Macaluso and Mason. For some reason, they did not seem to like me too well. We studied Julius Caesar, and then we turned in our "Critiques". Mr. Lindner had announced on the first day of class that he never flunked anyone. He gave out three grades: A, B and C. C was tantamount to failure in his eyes, but not to the registrar's office. I got my paper back, and Mr. Lindner had given me a "C" written in red pencil, with a note scribbled beneath the grade.

· · ·

I went up to Mr. Lindner as the class ended and asked what he had written with his scribbling. I could not read it. He said, "You didn't write this. It reads like the blurb from a book jacket." I exclaimed somewhat excitedly, "I wrote this. I'll swear on a stack of bibles — I wrote this." But he would not believe it.

If truth be told, I had read the book, and I understood Dickens's style. He would start out with a story. One or more chapters later, he would start out with a different story. And he would repeat this technique until at some point within the novel, the stories and characters started to come together. In my critique, I had likened the technique to a series of disparate and separate copper cable wires that get wound together to make a unified whole.

This critique I had written at Eddie Hassid's house, on Eddie Hassid's typewriter. I think Mr. Lindner had stipulated that the critique must be type-written, and we did not have a typewriter. But I never consulted Eddie or anyone else about what to write in the critique. I don't even think I showed it to Eddie, nor his younger brother Andy. Eddie lived close, within walking distance, of the Mitchells, my mother's friends.

Difficult for me even to remember what else I did that fall of 1962. I do know that I showed up for band practice at 8 AM. And I remember that in Geometry, our official teacher was Mrs. McBean, an elderly lady who had been our family friend Bob Habeeb's geometry teacher when he went to

Lowell in 1950. But Mrs. McBean turned over the class to a student teacher, who I thought was excellent.

I went to our Lowell High football games played in Kezar Stadium. Kezar was the same stadium that housed the San Francisco 49er football team in the NFL. Why I went to the games was because I played clarinet in the pep band. We played "On, On Cardinal" and "Muskrat Ramble" among other tunes. Ms. Carolyn Brash was my homeroom teacher. She was pro sports and pro Lowell High School, pointing out that New York Giants lineman Jack Stroud was a Lowell graduate and had been one of her students.

We had on our Lowell team Bob Lee at quarterback and Tim McAteer, and Louie Curtman as backfield mates. Reeves Moses was our wide end. Bob Lee actually made it to the NFL, playing backup for years before leaving to do something else. Bob Lee's mom had been a secretary at the St. Francis Episcopal church, so I sort of knew her. She was not kind to me, nor was she by any means nasty with me. She was there with her red hair.

Our band leader at Lowell High School was the legendary Mr. Reginald Krieger. Mr. Krieger was past his prime when I went there. Actually, Mr. Krieger being the director was one of the reasons I wanted to go to Lowell in the first place. I guess years earlier, Krieger had been an outstanding trumpet player, somebody that our Junior High director, Marv Nelson held in high esteem. From what I learned, Mr. Krieger had demonstrated to a statewide convention playing music on a bunch of sea kelp, to which he had attached his trumpet mouthpiece.

But Mr. Krieger's taste in music ran contrary to mine. He liked Broadway tunes, von Suppé, and Tchaikovsky. Mozart, Beethoven and Brahms were famous names to him. He had little understanding of their music, beyond Haydn's trumpet concerto. And so, at this stage of his career at Lowell, he preyed on all the student teachers who wanted to study with him. He turned over the conducting duties to them in large part. And none of the student teachers I experienced at Lowell went much beyond being merely competent.

I remember that fall, I received tickets to attend a rehearsal of the San Francisco Symphony. I recall being outside the hall at the San Francisco Civic Center, and as I was about to go in, I saw our geometry student teacher also about to attend the rehearsal. I said hello, he replied with a sincere hello, but he never smiled.

Inside the performance hall, I watched the conductor, Enrique Jorda, go through the Symphony No 9, "The Great" by Franz Schubert. This music was a complete revelation to me. No one had told me about this music. But Jorda rehearsed the first movement over and over again, so I got the full color and power of the brass section. When he jumped to the third movement, I was impressed by the strings in their sweeping melody. And then he rehearsed the Finale.

.   .   .

I rushed home to look up the descriptions of this work in my music anthology. And I read the story of the final symphony of Franz Schubert. My mother complained about Schubert, that he always wrote beautiful music, but he never knew how to end a piece. And to our good flutist at Lowell and the All City orchestra, Virginia Wilkins, I maintained that Schubert had written this final symphony at an age which Beethoven had not even written his first symphony. And that had Schubert lived, he would have become known as the greatest composer of all time. Virginia did not agree with me.

ELAINE

I guess I fell in love that fall, or perhaps later. In any event, in the two years I was to spend at Lowell High School, I was in love with a girl named Elaine Manos. I can never forget her. She always went around with a chubby Asian girl, whose name I never knew, or at least, have forgotten.

FALSELY ACCUSED AGAIN

One day, I was in study hall. And this girl, the friend of Elaine Manos, was substituting as the classroom monitor. Her duties included the taking of attendance. The regular "teacher" of the study hall was Mr. Drysdale, the baseball coach. One day, Mr. Drysdale called me up to his desk and told me I had to go to the Vice Principal's office because I had an unexplained absence on a certain day. That certain day happened to be the day when the substitute classroom monitor was taking attendance. I began to protest to Mr.

Drysdale. He replied, "Buddy, all I know is I looked over at your desk and you weren't there." I replied, "But Mr. Drysdale. You were not even in the classroom that day." After having pointed this out, Mr. Drysdale apologized and quickly dropped the request that I report to the Vice Principal's office.

STAN THE MAN

In gym class, I remember I was mixed in with seniors. Our teacher was a Mr. Stan Stewart, who coached the JV basketball squad. For some reason, Stewart took to calling me Pal-LAY, to rhyme with ballet. Now my last name was still spelled Pallett, no "e" on the end. I had not yet added the "e" so people often mispronounced my name. That fall, Stewart had us line up across the road from the new high school grounds. There was a kind of "cross-country" course that he instructed us to run.

I knew that back in the 7th grade in Phoenix, Arizona, I had trained extensively as a distance runner. But in the later places I had lived, I had not run at all. Yet, I took to the long distance run with great enthusiasm, and by the half-way mark, I was in the lead. But then came a hill climb. After climbing the hill, I was exhausted, and I had to stop. I remember a husky kid named Terry passed me then and I started to walk the rest of the way. Meanwhile, a dozen or so guys ran past me. And I finished in a trot, still not able to catch my breath.

Phil, playing his new Buffet clarinet with Uncle
David on piano, and Cousin Olivia on flute.
Stonestown, December 1962

I attended the fall concert of the All-City orchestra, which I was about to join. They started off playing Rossini's overture to L'italiana in Algeri. The work has a pretty exposed and difficult oboe part. The thing I remember today about this concert is that the oboe player screwed up his descending staccato part. He had two chances at it, and he screwed it up both times. Don't let anyone tell you that if someone doesn't come through on the performance stage okay, people will forget about it. No, that is wrong. I will never forget how this poor guy playing the oboe screwed up his part. I will give him an "A" for effort.

EPILOGUE

IN THE COMING YEARS, I would leave the West Coast forever. The future, which I will report in my next book, includes my move to New York, and my eventual move to Berlin, Germany.

NOTES

1. SAN FRANCISCO – IN THE BEGINNING

1. http://web.archive.org/web/20220324202846/https://www.thepeoplehistory.com/1950.html
2. https://www.theburningofrome.com/advices/what-was-happening-in-the-mid-1950s/

2. VASHON ISLAND, WASHINGTON – A LITTLE BOY LOST

1. www.thepeoplehistory.com›1952.html
www.cbinsights.com›research›startup-failure-post-mortem
frontierplayhouse.blogspot.com›2015›05›wild-bill-hickok-series-on.html

3. VASHON ISLAND – A LITTLE BOY LOVED

1. annkoplow.wordpress.com›2018›05›07›day-1953-1953

4. ST. ANDREWS HOUSE – HOODS CANAL, WASHINGTON

1. https://www.infoplease.com/year/1954

5. EDMONDS, WASHINGTON – SARGE THE DOG

1. https://www.thepeoplehistory.com/1955.html

6. CALIFORNIA, HERE I COME - LOOKING FOR A HOME

1.   https://www.infoplease.com/year/1956

7. MILL VALLEY, CALIFORNIA - THAT'S MY HOME?

1.   https://www.thepeoplehistory.com/1957.html

8. CORTE MADERA, CALIFORNIA - STILL IN MARIN COUNTY

1.   https://www.thepeoplehistory.com/1958.html

9. PHOENIX, ARIZONA - LITTLE LEAGUE LOST

1.   https://www.babyboomers.com/1959

10. EDMONDS, WASHINGTON - COULD HAVE BEEN CHICAGO

1.   **https://www.thepeoplehistory.com/1960s.html**

11. SAN FRANCISCO - MY HEART DIDN'T SEEM TO MATTER

1.   **https://www.babyboomers.com/1961**

12. THE CLARINET BECOMES MY NICHE

1.   **https://www.thepeoplehistory.com/1962.html**

ABOUT THE AUTHOR

Philip B Pallette is an emerging author of basketball stories and couples therapy. This is Philip's second book. His first was a biography of the 1930s legendary basketball Hall of Fame star, Hank Luisetti.